Now there were dwelling in Jerusalem Jews, devout men from every nation under heaven. And at this sound the multitude came together, and they were bewildered, because each one heard them speaking in his own language. And they were amazed and wondered, saying, "Are not all these who are speaking Galileans? And how is it that we hear, each of us in his own native language? . . . We hear them telling in our own tongues the mighty works of God." And all were amazed and perplexed, saying to one another, "What does this mean?"

ACTS OF THE APOSTLES 2:5FF.

To Elizabeth + Keith

from

Bisola + Busola

Blessings .

Whose Religion Is Christianity?

THE GOSPEL BEYOND THE WEST

Lamin Sanneh

William B. Eerdmans Publishing Company
Grand Rapids, Michigan / Cambridge, U.K.

Wm. B. Eerdmans Publishing Co.

255 Jefferson Ave. S.E., Grand Rapids, Michigan 49503 /
P.O. Box 163, Cambridge CB3 9PU U.K.

Printed in the United States of America

08 07 06 05 04   7 6 5 4 3

Library of Congress Cataloging-in-Publication Data

Sanneh, Lamin O.
Whose religion is Christianity? / Lamin Sanneh.
p.   cm.
Includes bibliographical references and index
ISBN 0-8028-2164-2 (pbk.)
1. Christianity — Developing countries — Miscellanea.
I. Title.
BR115.U6S26   2003

270.8′3 — dc21

2003060010

www.eerdmans.com

To the memory of my mother
And to that of other victims of cultural oppression

Not as we knew them any more,
Toilworn, and sad with burdened care —
Erect, clear-eyed, upon their brows
Thy name they bear.

Free from the fret of mortal years,
And knowing now Thy perfect will,
With quickened sense and heightened joy,
They serve Thee still.

Nor know to what high purpose Thou
Dost yet employ their ripened powers,
Nor how at Thy behest they touch
This life of ours.

Contents

vii

CONTENTS

Acknowledgments

My thanks go to many people who encouraged me in the writing of this book, including the many students I have had the privilege to know at the two academic institutions where I have spent most of my professional career: Harvard and Yale. I invited and received in discussions and writing criticisms of the subject of Christianity as a world religion, and used those to frame the broad terms of the interview approach. I made sure to throw away nothing of value in the criticisms, requiring only that they relate in some fashion to the subject itself. I had no idea at the time that such criticisms would one day become a significant part of the subject itself rather than remaining hidden and unacknowledged, but it shows the remarkable acuity of the students, not to mention my own good fortune, that their interventions should stand the test of time. They gave me quality education, it turned out, and that without charge.

I have profited greatly from colleagues in the secular disciplines and across many borders and persuasions. World Christianity has as yet developed little of the departmental or disciplinary prerogatives that frame conversations in the guild, and so it is natural to take advantage of the work of scholars not normally encountered outside their accepted fields. Perhaps one day world Christianity will acquire its own turf rights, but if that means an end to conversation, I hope that day remains in the distant future. Friends and colleagues have awakened me to the value of open-ended conversation.

I spoke with profit at many institutions and conferences where, with generous encouragement, I tried the interview approach. The decision to develop that into a book is due to my experience at several such public presentations. I learned in those settings that people desire to see connections made between academic ideas and public interest. Academics, too, weary all too easily with hearing lectures, and instead appreciate being an acknowledged part of the audience. I took that as a rebuke of the tendency of talking shop and as a challenge to make conversation a common endeavor. Nothing is more important than making oneself understandable and engaging, and no method is better at that than one that includes the audience in the conversation. In the interview style, I discovered, I became part of the audience, not lecturing only but conversing also, and affirming common ownership of the subject.

The work and counsel of many people have helped deepen my understanding of the subject, among them:

Acknowledgments

Ken Goodpasture, Lesslie Newbigin, Stanley Samartha, and Harold Turner, all now of blessed memory; Jacob Ajayi, John Carman, Harvey Cox, Richard Niebuhr, Diana Eck, William Hutchison, Paul Hanson, Gordon Kaufman, Kenneth Cragg, Andrew Walls, Paul Gifford, Meg Guider, Carol Delany, Peter Paris, Bill Burrows, Edith Blumhoeffer, Albrecht Hauser, Hans Haafkens, Patrick Ryan, S.J., Ian Maclain, Dale Irwin, Jacob Olupona, Todd Hartch, Lewis Rambo, Moonjang Lee, Kwame Bediako, Bill O'Brien, James Phillips, Jonathan Bonk, and Robert Frickenberg. I wish to acknowledge in particular the interest and encouragement of Jon Pott, David Burke, and Richard Gray, who all read the manuscript in draft and made valuable suggestions. Without hesitation, Jon Pott agreed to move forward with the manuscript to publication. I have enjoyed and learned much from colleagues at Yale, particularly Lee Keck, Gene Outka, Owen Fiss, and Michael Holquist. My indebtedness to all these people, however, carries no implications of responsibility on their part, I should stress.

The fond spirit of Nunu, my long-deceased mother, broods over this work. She suffered much affliction, abuse, and neglect in her straitened, yet unstinting life that itself was cut short by an unnecessary and untimely death. She found scant shade amidst the acacia thornbushes of her affliction. Yet, instead of wearing her down, adversity seemed to refine her as she poured out her life to sustain her family, to honor her friends, and to cherish all. I can only with grief imagine her sorrow now if she knew the slow progress made to improve the lot of her fellow clanswomen still languishing under the intolerable burdens that broke her. May the Blessed Mother be the valiant defender of her cause and give shade to those who, like her, are without hope and without ally.

From conversations in the home and around the dinner table I received much enlightenment from my family. K often has used humor and wit to deflate the overblown, and Sia's organized focus has shown how multitasking can be done without too much risk of tripping. Sand has shown me what a structured day should look like from an unhastled, commodious view of time. The book is a tribute to the spirit of familial conversation that has sustained us over the years, and with deep gratitude to them, I offer it now to the reader in that spirit of mutual sharing.

Christianity Uncovered: The Discovery of the Gospel beyond the West

Receding Horizons

The current worldwide Christian resurgence has prompted fresh skepticism across departments, institutions, and disciplines, skepticism about the nature, scope, outcome, and implications of Christian growth and expansion. Many writers argue that we live in a post-Christian West, and that, thanks to irreversible secularization, we have outlived the reigning convictions of a once Christian society. They are skeptical about a new resurgence, and remind us that we are people who, with melancholy foreboding, once brooded on our end but are now no longer so preoccupied. We remember our coming of age on the fateful occasion when the devil, who had stalked us all through our childhood, finally committed suicide from having witnessed the impregnable achievements of science and technology. That potent moment

ushered in the era of modern humanity, and with it immense liberal gains. It sealed the fate of Christianity, except, that is, Christianity as individual piety without the
element of fear to oppress and condemn. The kingdom of
mammon accomplished the end of the kingdom of
heaven, and so with the fruits of science and enterprise
the European world can forgo with equanimity the threats
and promises of eternal life. So much, then, for the
church as a relevant institution. Along with other traditional symbols, the church is no longer a dominant land-
mark on our expanding mental landscape, even without
the reproach of current scandals about pedophile Catholic
priests and the cover-up. After all, the scandal of Santa
Claus debauching children to give them nightmares still
lacks the potency of the devil's sway over our eternal fate.

Such a secular mood swing, we are cautioned, does
not bode well for the prospects of a worldwide Christian
resurgence being welcome in the West. Skeptics look to
globalization to neutralize the religious resurgence, or
else to a combative Islam to challenge it at its source. But
in any case, the secular triumph of democratic liberalism
represents the evolutionary process of discredited religion. After the dust has settled, religion will leave the
field to its rightful secular successor.

Skeptics contend that if the story of the worldwide
Christian resurgence is to be told in the West, it will have
to make do with the snatches of rare attentiveness a
clamorous secular culture allows to a waning residual piety. The subject of world Christianity should otherwise be
allowed to slip quietly behind a cloud of benign neglect.

A Stream in Spate

The contemporary confidence in the secular destiny of the West as an elevated stage of human civilization is matched by the contrasting evidence of the resurgence of Christianity as a world religion; they are like two streams flowing in opposite directions. Perhaps the two currents have more in common than meets the eye, as if the impetus of secularization is set to fill the void from which religion has been drained, while religious resurgence elsewhere makes headway in societies not yet captured by secularism. No matter. What is at issue now is the surprising scale and depth of the worldwide Christian resurgence, a resurgence that seems to proceed without Western organizational structures, including academic recognition, and is occurring amidst widespread political instability and the collapse of public institutions, part of what it means to speak of a post-Western Christianity. Even church leaders have been unable to comprehend fully, still less to respond effectively to, the magnitude of the resurgence. In some areas it's like being hit by a tidal wave and unable to hold your footing. The fact is, no amount of institutional organizing can cope with the momentum. There necessarily will have to be ad hoc staging posts and a good deal of unconventional religious rehousing of converts until the pace slackens and the churches can catch their breath.

We have been given intimations of what is afoot in the world by the growing presence in the towns and cities of the West of members of new religious movements. In places as varied as Moscow, Paris, Amsterdam, Glasgow, London, New York, Atlanta, Washington, D.C., Chicago, and Los Angeles, new charismatic healing churches have sprouted as the far-flung offshoots of the worldwide Christian resurgence. We often learn about these religious groups from civic and law enforcement authorities being summoned to a neighborhood following complaints from irate neighbors of shouts, chanting, and other commotion emanating from prayer chapels. Is God so deaf that you need bedlam to rouse him, people ask indignantly? The wooden charge of disturbing the public peace in such situations seems inappropriate, yet our public officials seem lost for an answer. The churches and other religious institutions seem to fare no better. According to the order of things, religion, tolerated as a social indiscretion, should be allowed to go out with the Sunday twilight. Only people who don't know any better would behave differently.

Room for Difference

The new skepticism prompted by Christian resurgence requires us to close the gap between a robust secularism and a quiescent private piety in order to tell the story of Christianity as a world religion. To do that, I have decided to relate religion to secularism in an interactive, question-and-answer style. We should by this method be able to avoid the pitfalls of theological contextualization in which "context" determines what we value and do not value in religion. Context is not passive but comes preloaded with its own biases, ready to contest whatever claims it encounters. Contexts, after all, are constructed strategies. As such, a context-sensitive approach should be responsive without being naive. Therefore, we should look at religion in its own right. A way to do that is to stress religious intentions and the related signs, rites, and symbols. Another way is to pay attention to what religious people think and how they act. Thoughts, intentions, and actions together constitute the personal dimension of religion, while institutions, structures, and organizations constitute the social and public dimensions.

The interactive interview style tries to get at the personal dimension of religion, including the divergent views people have about the subject. Readers should feel unfettered enough by this interactive method to bring their own questions and concerns to the subject and to use the responses to develop, sharpen, or clarify their own ideas. The interview method should facilitate discussion, debate, and exchange without getting people defensive, and may be used as a framework for tackling difference in a charitable spirit and for discussing concrete issues in diverse contexts with mutual openness and respect.

It may be useful to identify the principles and rules that inform this approach. First, religion is not only suited to the interview method but is actually enhanced by it. People often think religion creates closed minds that see difference in terms of intolerance and division. Yet difference can be enriching and mutually instructive, while religion can be reassuring and ironic at the same time. For example, you may sometimes do God's will only by denying your own. Discernment is a fruit of obedience, and a gift of genuine solidarity. Choice is empty without it. Second, disagreement is not a barrier to dialogue. On the contrary, it is a test of the willingness to presume on each other's goodwill and to covet the best for each other. To be charitable is to be deserving of charity oneself. Without difference dialogue would be moot. If you feel the need to conceal what you believe for fear of difference, then dialogue becomes just a show, and agreement an illusion. Indeed, agreement by concealment is intolerance by another name, if truth be told.

An important issue in the literature on dialogue is thus often confused by the view that difference is threatening, fanatical, harmful, and negative while uniform agreement is sound, inclusive, and enlightened. If that were true, we would all be condemned to sameness, uniformity, and conformity. Yet even then we would not escape the threat, the intolerance, the feuding and the cursing that disagreement is supposed to cause. In light of intercommunal conflicts, intrafamily feuds, and the truculence that often arise in the same race, household, or national or faith community, we arrive at a pretty pass when we approach the world in defiance of difference, or in a misguided optimism about agreement. As Ogden Nash (1902-71) put it in one of his poems, "One would be in less danger / From the wiles of a stranger / If one's own kin and kith / Were more fun to be with." People often fight because they want the same thing, or make peace because they embrace difference.

Can Secularism Transcend Itself?

I have used this view of difference and diversity to develop and present the subject of Christianity as a world religion. Religion is too pervasive to restrict to personal habit or preference, even though personal conviction is a central aspect of the matter. Religion is already so entangled with our roots that it would be flying in the face of reality to try to deny it or claim it for one side only, or to reduce it to personal whim merely. The worldwide Christian resurgence is proof of the religion transcending ethnic, national, and cultural barriers. A new Christian encounter with secularism is occurring across those frontiers of ethnic, national, and cultural identity, and the outcome there will be affected as much by external forces as by internal ones. Accordingly, in spite of its impregnable roots in secular autonomy, individualism will likely be modified by the communicative realities of cross-cultural encounter.[1] Social relatedness will in all likeli-

---

1. In a spirited essay in the *Atlantic Monthly*, David Brooks, a news commentator and senior editor of the *Weekly Standard*, writes that secularism represents an incorrect reading of religion, that society does not get less religious as it grows richer and more educated. As proof, he says the denominations that have grown are those that have repudiated enlightened secularism, with decline in those churches that stand on the side of progress and modernity. In 1942 the *Atlantic Monthly* published an article predicting the end of the Christian church. In October 2002 the same magazine published an article describing the new global Christian resurgence. Brooks expresses frustration at "secular fundamentalists who are content to re-

hood prevail over emancipated individualism, and for once, secularism may transcend itself by encountering in the worldwide Christian resurgence the milieu of its own genesis.

In turning to that genesis, it transpires that the secular option may not be foreign to Christianity after all, but may represent an impetus of the religion from its original conception when a line was drawn between God and Caesar (Mark 12:17; Matt. 22:21) and believers were enjoined to pin their hopes on the kingdom of another world. In that world Caesar's sword could not do God's bidding. Secularization as a soft option was how the religion, after it had fallen for the fruits of Caesar's bidding, came to be divested of the warrants of state power. Soft secularization achieved two ends simultaneously: (a) it enshrined the sovereign rule of conscience in matters of faith, and (b) it established the limited role of government in society. In one move religion was freed of the burden of public enforcement, and government of the burden of divine entitlement. It was a double liberation the result of which, at least in the United States, was liberal democracy, a checkered and indirect offspring of the two-kingdom teaching. America was for a time spared the secular excesses of revolutionary France, and instead of becoming the Napoleon of the New World, George

---

main smugly ignorant of enormous shifts occurring all around them. . . . A great Niagara of religious fervor is cascading down around them while they stand obtuse and dry in the little cave of their own parochialism." David Brooks, "Kicking the Secularist Habit: A Six-Step Program," *Atlantic Monthly*, March 2003, 26-27.

Washington became an icon of freedom, his modesty the antidote to megalomania. "I have the consolation to believe," Washington said in his farewell address in 1796, "that while choice and prudence invite me to quit the political scene, patriotism does not forbid it."

In the French case, a hard-edged secularism emerged and acquired a life of its own, with state jurisdiction expanding to make religion subordinate. God was privatized and displaced by the national state as the source of truth and as an object of worship. ("The nation exists before all, it is the origin of everything . . . it is the law itself," said Abbé Sieyès in 1789.) At any rate, secularism promoted civic religion to produce a comprehensive doctrine of public reason. Armed now with state power, secularism became combative. Religion was cut down as a private option and given dubious legal protection as a suspect contender for the rights of man, rather than being an inalienable right necessitating a curb on state power. Religious opponents in turn became combative and forgot that separation was a religious safeguard in the first place.

Perhaps in the worldwide Christian resurgence we can overcome this polarization by recalling the circumstances that gave birth to the church as a divine office rather than as a political institution, enabling the church to flourish in spite of every attempt by the state to suppress it. Whatever the excesses of secularism as a political ideology, secularization as a cultural process does not seem to be at odds with the religious resurgence of today. One sign of this is that the contemporary religious resurgence is taking place in spite of state weakness, and often in spite of state suppression, rather than because of state support. Except in a few notable cases, secularization has shed its hard-core tendency of drawing on the prerogatives of state power to become a combative dogma. Religion has space to flourish.

Indigenous Discovery: Ground Rules on Home Ground

I have decided to give priority to indigenous response and local appropriation over against missionary transmission and direction, and accordingly have reversed the argument by speaking of the *indigenous discovery of Christianity* rather than the *Christian discovery of indigenous societies*. The language factor is central to the indigenous cause, as the work of Bible translation shows. The language aspect of traditional culture provides a useful and illuminating way of overcoming the obstacle that evolutionary theory has placed in the path of taking seriously religion's impact on history and society. The fact that Bible translation adopted into its canon the indigenous names for God implied at the minimum a tacit rejection of the standard monotheism-polytheism dichotomy of evolutionary thought, and opened the way for indigenous innovation and motivation in the religious life. Accordingly, Olorun, the Yoruba high god, was adopted into Christianity with little diminution of his epiphanies in the Orisa as lesser divinities.

Bible translation has thus helped to bring about a historic shift in Christianity's theological center of gravity by pioneering a strategic alliance with local conceptions of religion. This indigenous theological domestication is comparable in scope and consequence to the Hellenization of theology in the early church, but this time without the state apparatus. It is difficult to overestimate the implications of this indigenous change for the future shape of the religion, and for the global prospects of "third wave" democratization in the affected societies.[2]

To Write to Serve the Reader

Numerous helpful studies continue to call our attention to issues arising from the worldwide Christian resurgence. This book, however, will not discuss the scope of what scholars and students have written on the subject, but will instead try to interact with the reader for whom busyness is a necessary evil and time a precious commodity. Many ideas and views will be presented in a succinct summary fashion, which entails taking liberties with nuance and niceties in order to be responsive. The payoff should be brevity, clarity, and dispatch. This should hasten the discussion along without being precipitous or evasive. I will attempt to strike a balance between the personal spirit of daily encounter and the conven-

2. Samuel P. Huntington, *The Third Wave: Democratization in the Late Twentieth Century* (Norman: University of Oklahoma Press, 1991), 72ff.

tions of the written page. Hard questions will be pressed without turning the interrogation into an inquisition, and similarly, good-faith answers will be offered without smug complacency. The dialogue will be set at a varied pace to avoid padding and circularity but, it is my hope, without being tight-lipped or impetuous.

The book is written in a freestyle way but with a built-in structure. The reader can join the conversation at any point without feeling disjointed. The questions will not merely be formal but instead will represent substantial angles on the subject matter. Perspective is important, and the more diverse the better. The responses, for that reason, will try to keep close to the questions, and in that way to leave space for rejoinders. By its very nature a conversation is informal, though writing it down requires a certain formality. In recognition of that, I will number the individual questions and provide subject subheadings to give the reader a tracking device. As a further precaution, field practice rather than theory will be the controlling principle of the discussion. I hope in that and in other ways the book will serve the reader rather than the reader serving the book. The reader should be able to enter into the conversation and contribute something of his or her own to the exchange. There are material gaps to be filled, to be sure, but what is more important and desirable is to have the reader participate in a nuanced conversation about the discovery of Christianity beyond the well-trodden paths of the West. No special background or initiation is required to engage fully in this exchange, and to become a standing partner in the cause.

CHAPTER ONE

The Wind Blows Where It Wills: Christianity as a World Religion

FERMENT, RENEWAL, AND PLURALISM IN WORLD CHRISTIANITY

The old spells of benign quality lent themselves very easily as a bridge between paganism and Christianity in the days of groping from belief to belief. The old pagans of my time had seen the emissaries of the new faith working ruthlessly against their loved ancestors in the earlier days of missionary work, and for that reason most of them resisted to the very end every effort to christianize them. But they distinguished with extraordinary sensitiveness between the new God and His human prophets. Their stubborn resistance was not directed against the notion of a foreign deity but against the church organization as such. The Christian God seemed very powerful to them. Had He not saved from the anger of their own spirits the desecrators of their village shrines? They had need of the protection of such a Power, not His enmity, in their bitter loss.

ARTHUR GRIMBLE[1]

Part I: The Facts on the Ground

By 2002 Christian expansion continued to gather momentum, and the churches in Africa and Asia, for example, were bursting at the seams with an uninterrupted influx of new members. Yet we were told as late as the 1970s to expect a steady decline in Christian numbers by 2000, with the resurgence of Islam sealing the fate of the church. For example, at Edinburgh 1910 the ecumenical conference was told by J. R. Mott to expect Africa to be taken over by Islam. So the expansion of Christianity at the end of the twentieth century has come as something of a surprise, and we need to examine the reasons for this expansion and what indications there are of a transition to a new era of the history of Christianity. New communities have embraced Christianity, with implications for a fresh understanding of the gospel in world history.

The facts of the expansion are little in dispute: Africa, for example, in 1900, by which time the continent had come firmly under colonial rule, had 8.7 million Christians, about 9 percent of the total population of 107.86

---

1. Grimble, *A Pattern of Islands*, 120. The description is of the Gilbert and Ellice Islands in the Pacific in the early 1900s.

million. The majority of the Christians were Coptic and Ethiopian Orthodox. Muslims in 1900 outnumbered Christians by a ratio of nearly 4:1, with some 34.5 million, or 32 percent of the population. In 1962 when Africa had largely slipped out of colonial control, there were about 60 million Christians, with Muslims at about 145 million. Of the Christians, 23 million were Protestants and 27 million were Catholics. The remaining 10 million were Coptic and Ethiopian Orthodox.

By 1985 it had become clear that a major expansion of Christianity had been under way in Africa in spite of prevailing pessimism about the imminent collapse of postindependent states, and of waning confidence in the church in Europe. Although they were little prepared for it, the churches found themselves as the only viable structures remaining after the breakdown of state institutions, and as such had to shoulder a disproportionate burden of the problems of their societies. Ironically, Christian Africans came predominantly from the poor and marginalized. By 1985 there were over 16,500 conversions a day, yielding an annual rate of over 6 million. In the same period (i.e., between 1970 and 1985), some 4,300 people were leaving the church on a daily basis in Europe and North America. A good deal of the evidence for Christian growth in Africa was available in sources from the U.N. and elsewhere, such as *Europa Sourcebook,* but the significance of the data was lost on much of the world.[2]

2. See *World Christian Handbook,* ed. H. Wakelin Coxill and Sir Kenneth Grubb (London: Lutterworth, 1967); *World Christian Encyclo-*

The world, however, was in no mood to receive good news about Christianity, not least because it was coming from Africa. A public consensus, shared by many Christians, had emerged that a tolerant and inclusive secular world required the abandonment of Christian exclusivism. The chief offenders here were missions, but in the logic of historical irony, through the self-righteous zeal of missionaries to win converts, Christianity exhausted itself and so could be sidelined in the march toward a more open and tolerant world. Public objection to mission was reinforced by a corresponding prickliness at the slightest suggestion of cultural insensitivity to non-Western cultures. A rule for measuring tolerance became the degree to which one was opposed to Christian exclusivism and to mission, or, the other side of the coin, the degree to which one was least likely to be accused of cultural insensitivity, a fate to be avoided at all costs. All that was needed for the inclusive brigade to storm the walls of a residual Christianity was for members of other religions and cultures to cry insensitivity to the indigenous culture. The new world order, secular or pluralist, was constructed on an inclusivism uncompromised by

---

pedia: A Comprehensive Survey of Churches and Religions in the Modern World, ed. David B. Barrett, George T. Kurian, and Todd M. Johnson, 2nd ed., 2 vols. (New York: Oxford University Press, 2001), vol. 1, The World by Countries: Religionists, Churches, Ministries, vol. 2, The World by Segments: Religions, Peoples, Languages, Cities, Topics. Michael J. McClymond, "Making Sense of the Census, or, What 1,999,563,838 Christians Might Mean for the Study of Religion," Journal of the American Academy of Religion, vol. 70, no. 4, December 2002, 875-90.

Christianity. If the religion survived, it should be as a facet of the triumph of secular faith, or not all. A blanket secular inclusivism turned out to have exclusivist religious holes — yet another irony.

With their reputation and high visibility in the field, mainline missions were left with little choice but to beat a retreat in the face of this public mistrust. But the corollary of the comprehensive decline of Christianity failed to follow from the end of colonialism and of mainline missions. Instead, Christian numbers grew at a much faster rate than ever before, confounding critic and supporter alike. Still, having taken the position that Christianity constituted the sole barrier to tolerance, critics played the ostrich when faced with contrary evidence, insisting that the conversions were other than what they were, and that in any case a terrifying descent into intolerance was threatened with the new "global" Christianity.

Accordingly, stories about a resurgent Christianity in Africa and elsewhere fell on deaf ears. If people needed an excuse, they could point to the call for a moratorium on missions that went out in the 1970s from the All Africa Council of Churches, putting churches in Europe and North America on the defensive. Noninterference was the official policy, and with it a scrupulous distancing from events in the field. It is also a fact that there was a considerable gap between the African Christian leaders calling for a moratorium on missions and the mass of new Christians converting in droves, with the effect that local Christian groundswells lacked an outlet for publicity and recognition. Political correctness created a PR vacuum.

Yet, as I said, the facts of the expansion of Christianity are little in dispute. It is their significance that requires explanation. One major factor is how this expansion has taken place *after* colonialism and during the period of national awakening. Perhaps colonialism was an obstacle to the growth of Christianity, so that when colonialism ended it removed a stumbling block. A second factor was the delayed effect of Bible translation into African languages. With vernacular translation went cultural renewal, and that encouraged Africans to view Christianity in a favorable light. A third factor was African agency. Africans stepped forward to lead the expansion without the disadvantage of foreign compromise. Young people, especially women, were given a role in the church.

Another factor little noticed in the statistics is a theological one: Christian expansion was virtually limited to those societies whose people had preserved the indigenous name for God. That was a surprising discovery, because of the general feeling that Christianity was incompatible with indigenous ideas of religion. Yet the apparent congruity between Christianity and the indigenous name for God finds a parallel in the fact of Christian expansion occurring *after* rather than during colonialism. In any case, Africans best responded to Christianity where the indigenous religions were strongest, not weakest, suggesting a degree of indigenous compatibility with the gospel, and an implicit conflict with colonial priorities.

The Islamic comparison, however brief, may be helpful here, and for reasons not just of cultural sensitivity. Muslim expansion and growth, which occurred, were most impressive in areas where the indigenous religions, particularly as organized cults, had been vanquished or else subjugated, and where local populations had either lost or only vaguely remembered their name for God. For this reason colonialism as a secularizing force helped to advance Muslim gains in Africa. Colonial administrators shared a low regard for African religions with Muslim scholars, which helped suppress local cults and advance Islam's public standing.

The end of colonial rule inhibited the expansion of Islam in Africa, whereas the opposite seems to have happened with Christianity. The colonial system was schizoid about Christianity. The religion represented the West's moral superiority over tribal superstition, but missions and their vernacular emphasis confused the issue by allowing a naturalized Christianity to take root and to foment local subversion. Fearing Israelite sentiments of liberation, administrators accordingly clamped down on the new Christian movements, threatening their followers and sympathizers with reprisals and rounding up and incarcerating their leaders. Muslim leaders, for their part, opposed Christianity for their own reasons, not least because they considered it no less idolatrous than African religions. The three gods they ascribed to Christian teaching were no less scandalous than the many gods of pagan worship. In the postcolonial era, Muslim leaders turned to political agitation to push Islam's public agenda. Hence the turmoil in Muslim ranks about pressing the case for shari'ah law as penal law, and for filling the vacuum of public morality from which Christianity has been driven.

A word may be in order here about the Christian response to the Muslim political turmoil. Christian Africans, like their counterparts in the West, were little prepared for Islamic radicalism, and saw it as an *Eintagesfliege*, what the Germans call a bothersome fly that dies after a brief day of glory. But the persistent Muslim turmoil revealed the strategic weakness of a privatized Christianity unschooled in the science of government and unprotected against the negative fallout of consensual politics. A privatized Christianity seemed in fact to have emboldened religious radicalism. Radicals blame it for its tolerance of moral compromises that have weakened society just as Europeans attack it for liberal setbacks. It is little surprise that the new churches have been left scrambling for a way out of this maze: impossible at the same time to answer radical calls for collective discipline and liberal demands for individual freedom. All this has been fortuitously compounded by the sudden and mass influx of converts into Christianity, leaving the churches reeling under the weight, if we may return to the subject. Motives more powerful than self-preservation must lie at the basis of becoming a Christian in these conditions of acute challenge and ironic misunderstanding.

*　　*

A skeptical Western audience, fortified with anthropological theory and with a postcolonial sensitivity, will scarcely budge from its view of Christian mission as cultural imperialism and religious bigotry. Besides, developing societies as the new frontier of world Christianity strikes many as far-fetched. If, in the language of nineteenth-century science, the natives consumed themselves in ancestral rites without any measurable effect on their character but instead remained stranded in enchanted jungle haunts, why in heaven's name should the world trust them when they step forward under a Christian banner (see sec. VII below)? In a roundtable discussion those attitudes could be explored and perhaps satisfactorily resolved. It is hard to do that in an essay format, shackled as it is by constraints of demonstrative argument and accompanying annotated referencing. Yet because one is dealing with attitudes rather than with matters of information and sources, it is necessary to depart from the essay style for another that calls for an interactive engagement characteristic of the question-and-answer style. The evidence I wish to marshal must now be deployed in response to a range of concerns and demands. Let us now shift to that interview format to deal with Christianity as a world religion in its own right.

Part II: World Christianity and Christendom: Parallels and Divergences

Definitions

QUESTION I: Would you explain the words in the title of the chapter, "Ferment, Renewal, and Pluralism in World Christianity"? What do you mean by Christian ferment and renewal? Is that a euphemism for Christian triumphalism?

ANSWER: The ferment of Christianity is the spontaneous coming into being of Christian communities among populations that had not been Christian. It is not a euphemism for Christian triumphalism but a cause for action and a challenge to complacency.

QUESTION 2: What do you mean by renewal?

ANSWER: Christianity has caused a renewal of local languages, and the old customs and traditions in response to its ethics of love, reconciliation, justice, and responsibility. That renewal has also meant new structures and institutions guiding the expansion.

QUESTION 3: What do you mean by "world Christianity"? Is that the same as "global Christianity"?

ANSWER: "World Christianity" is the movement of Christianity as it takes form and shape in societies that previously were not Christian, societies that had no bureaucratic tradition with which to domesticate the gospel. In these societies Christianity was received and expressed through the cultures, customs, and traditions of the people affected. World Christianity is not one thing, but a variety of indigenous responses through more or less effective local idioms, but in any case without necessarily the European Enlightenment frame. "Global Christianity," on the other hand, is the faithful replication of Christian forms and patterns developed in Europe. It echoes Hilaire Belloc's famous statement, "Europe is the faith." It is, in fact, religious establishment and the cultural captivity of faith.

QUESTION 4: Does "global Christianity," then, compare with "Christendom"? What exactly is "Christendom"?[3]

ANSWER: "Christendom" refers to the medieval imperial phase of Christianity when the church became a domain of the state, and Christian profession a matter of political enforcement. Religious strife and conflict created shock waves of territorial upheaval, because wars of religion were wars of nations. Individual excommunication had its counterpart in the territorial interdict. The term "global Christianity" carries vestiges still of that root imperial phase by suggesting that growing communities of professing Christians around the world are evidence of the economic and political security interests of Europe, that churches everywhere are a religious expression of Europe's political reach, or else a reaction to it. "Global Christianity" as an expression also carries connotations of parallels with economic globalization, with the same forces of global trade and the Internet revolution fueling the spread of a seamless environment of information and exchange without borders. So, yes, in that sense "global Christianity" and "Christendom" are interchangeable. Today they are, however, anachronistic.

QUESTION 5: What caused this structural shift in world Christianity in the first place? What brought about the demise of institutional Christendom, of Christianity as a global, imperial mandate?

---

3. See Philip Jenkins, "A New Christendom," *Chronicle of Higher Education*, March 29, 2002.

ANSWER: The development of mother tongues as the means of receiving the gospel caused the shift. Under Christendom the basis and rationale for transmitting the gospel were colonial annexation and subjugation, with the church as an afterthought. Native lands and labor were expropriated, commercial and administrative agents appointed and deployed, mission stations set up, and church life and practice regulated. That way "Europeandom" as the faith and politics of early modern Europe spread abroad and was legitimized by the sacraments of the church. But with the shift into native languages, the logic of religious conversion assumed an internal dynamic, with a sharp turn away from external direction and control. Indigenizing the faith meant decolonizing its theology, and membership of the fellowship implied spiritual home rule. World Christianity was thereby weaned of the political habits of Christendom, even though the mental habits died hard. Consequently many writers in Europe and America, and some Third World theologians, continue to speak of "Christendom" as a political construct, with religion creating new political groupings marked by competition and rivalry.

QUESTION 6: Do you think missionaries had that indigenous shift in mind when they practiced vernacular translation? Weren't they in fact thinking of conversion as numerical rather than as indigenous empowerment? Wasn't the competitive motive driving them?

ANSWER: I don't think missionaries necessarily had in mind indigenous empowerment when they embarked on translation, and I think competition was an overriding motive of their actions. It is important, however, not to see missionaries as leaving such deep footprints that converts had little to do except trace them. Thus, whether or not we credit the missionaries with the positive effects of mother tongue deployment, we must still recognize its double-edged historical impact on indigenous cultures and on the "global" pretensions of Western Christianity. The strengthening of indigenous cultures is the kind of unforeseen fact that makes history interesting. The undisputed unintended consequences of actions are beyond the control of the actors themselves. History does not guarantee the future, nor, at the same time, does it evade it.

QUESTION 7: Even if we don't credit the missionaries for mother tongue mobilization, shouldn't we credit local agents and pioneers?

ANSWER: We should and we must. These local pioneers rose to the missionary challenge and took charge of the direction that mother tongue deployment indicated for Christianity and for their societies. An inculturated Christianity is not merely a sequel of discredited versions of the religion; it anticipates an emancipated society, a situation for which local leadership is best suited. Consequently the somewhat limited goal of Bible translation triggered a much broader process of ethnographic field research and historical documentation to produce a ripple effect on politics, economics, culture, and society, as well as on religion. That was the case in Hawaii where, for example, in the cause of translating the Bible, including documenting centuries of Hawaiian culture and history, the missionaries were the first to learn the language and to reduce it to writing. That today the language has survived at all is due almost entirely to the earlier work of Bible translation.[4]

Christian Origins, Local Feedback, and World Order Values

QUESTION 8: What is the significance of the growth of world Christianity for the West?

ANSWER: The West can encounter in the world Christian movement the gospel as it is being embraced by societies that had not been shaped by the Enlightenment, and so gain an insight into the culture that shaped the origins of the NT church. That might bring about a greater appreciation for the NT background of Christianity. It might also shed light on the issues the early church faced as it moved between the Jewish and Gentile worlds.

QUESTION 9: Yes, that may be interesting for religious scholars, but is it not distinctly possible that world Christianity will produce violent political cleavages with religion as a truculent impediment?

ANSWER: That possibility has been canvassed by some Western writers who speak of a coming Christendom that will seek to duplicate the cold war realignment of the world along medieval religious lines. These writers say the worldwide character of Christian profes-

---

4. "Churches Try to Protect Hawaii's Native Tongue," *The New York Times*, February 22, 2003.

sion will spawn a corresponding global ideology of power. A new age of Christian crusades in that scenario will compete with Muslim jihads to plunge the world into endemic warfare. In that brave new world the rack and fire of thirteenth-century Europe will be replaced by nuclear warheads and anthrax. A benign, humorous version of this macabre scenario is the spectacle of excitable tribes from the tropics turning up in Europe and North America as loin-clad emissaries to reevangelize the remnant. Because of the alleged conservative religious outlook of world Christianity, the reevangelization of the West would mean the wholesale overthrow of the liberal achievements of the modern West that would cause a relapse into intolerance. In other words, the post-Christian West should see in the rise of a post-Western world Christianity the potential for a major global cultural disruption and grave historical setback. Benign or not, global Christianity is not the occasion for complacency.

QUESTION 10: That sounds frightening, but is it a plausible scenario?

ANSWER: No, I don't think so, at least not on the basis of what we know. It's hard to see how world Christianity, which has become the religious reality it is today without an accompanying colonial political structure to propel it, should then be thrust forward as a crusading political ideology as Christendom. If, as is generally recognized, Christian expansion is occurring in societies marked by weak states and among impoverished populations, and where religious loyalties are stronger than political ones, then it seems fantastic to say such Christian expansion has the potential to generate structures of global political dominance in which political loyalties will be stronger than religious ones. It would take a strange alchemy to bring that about.

QUESTION 11: Why, then, do you think such predictions resonate so well in the West?

ANSWER: I agree it beggars the mind. Take South Africa, for example. You'll find little evidence there of the churches with global pretensions being aligned on a political fault line. The synod of African bishops, as another example, has committed itself to programs of social justice and reconstruction without a political blueprint. In other respects African Christianity is the consequence of haphazard, unorchestrated popular mobilization, much of it outside, or even against, mainstream bodies. African Christianity, then, is the irony of mass religious enthusiasm pitted against mass disenchantment with the political structures. It evokes the situation of NT Christianity, as I said. A Christendom analysis, however, remains attractive in a post–cold war era still attuned to danger and threats. The grim prognosis also fits well with the secular view that religion has had a negative role in the checkered story of human progress. That view may be justified in light of the mixed history of Western Christendom and of the dim prospects for Christianity in the West. Still, the experience of a cold war–hardened West that is now in its religious twilight is unreliable for tracking the course of a dawning post-Western world Christianity. At any rate, it should make us pause that most historians of the subject have not advanced such a grim prognosis. The past is not a secure guide for the future.

QUESTION 12: But hasn't Christianity as organized religion always worked hand in glove with the organized state? Why should world Christianity be a break from the tradition of state patronage?

ANSWER: Organized religion under state patronage has been a mixed bag, and has, as such, justifiably prompted protests in both Catholic and Protestant Christianity. Imperial protection was no less onerous, whether as favor or as obligation. Be that as it may, world Christianity is unarmed, and has been striking for its lack of political clout. Instead, it has been subjected to state-directed persecution. In the event, apart from calls for sacrificial national involvement, the new churches have been politically quiescent, or even acquiescent, and content to allow the faith to express itself as a privatized form of personal piety. The churches now face a different challenge, though, for confronted with low public confidence in state institutions, they need to break with the tradition of religious privatization in order to impact public ethics. Here they could take a leaf out of Christendom's book and offer institutional support with political clout. It's a tough choice, still, for political activism has as many pitfalls as religious privatization.

QUESTION 13: You spoke just now of the twilight of Europe in its religious phase. Is decline the only problem of the churches, or do you think the moral nerve has been touched?

ANSWER: I think there is something deeper. About

the decline, the statistics are unequivocal. But beneath and beyond that has been a strategic retreat into isolation where the spirit seems to be wilting. It has taken the form of a mood swing in which people have been preoccupied with taking stock, with the setting sun and lengthening shadows, with memorial armbands, with shades of gray, with requiem. As Sir Edward Grey declared, brooding on the dark clouds of his time, the lamps have gone out all over Europe. The religious imagination seems to have been hit with a bout of melancholy as it labors with strains of "Abide with me, fast falls the eventide" and "The Day Thou gavest, Lord, is ended, / The darkness falls at Thy behest." It's the solemn vespers without the Gloria, and is a far cry from the confident, robust tones of "Onward, Christian Soldiers," "The Son of God goes forth to war," or "Stand up, stand up for Jesus!" A dark, ominous drumbeat seems to rumble through the music of the filial hymn "God of our fathers, known of old . . . lest we forget, lest we forget."[5] It's as if Europeans have the Nunc Dimittis constantly on their lips, and so regret having to celebrate Christmas or Easter. Maybe too much history is a bad thing.

5. See Christopher Hitchens, "A Man of Permanent Contradictions," review of *The Long Recessional: The Imperial Life of Rudyard Kipling*, by David Gilmour, *Atlantic*, June 2002, 96-103.

Ancient Religious Stock and
Fresh Theological Advantage

QUESTION 14: I'd like to turn to the indigenous dimensions of world Christianity. You spoke earlier of adopting African names for God, saying that laid the basis for large-scale conversion. But I imagine much more is involved than mere statistics. What significance do you attach to African names for God and to their adoption in Christianity?

ANSWER: The name of God is basic to the structure of traditional societies. It forms and regulates agricultural rituals, territorial cults, agrarian festivals, the solar calendar, fertility ceremonies, mortuary observance, anniversary customs, units of generational measurement, naming rules, ethics, rank and status, gender relations, filial obligation, gift making, sacrificial offering, and so on. It's therefore hard to think of viable social systems without the name of God, but easy to envision societies that have become vulnerable because they lost the name or the sense of the transcendent. (Maybe there is a lesson for a post-Christian West here.)

It follows that the adoption of African names for God in Christianity would carry corresponding implications for social and cultural renewal, with effects on indigenous ethics and historical consciousness. We may summarize the matter as follows: the name of God contained ideas of personhood, economic life, and social/cultural identity; the name of God represented the indigenous theological advantage vis-à-vis missionary initiative. In that respect African religions as conveyers of the names of God were in relevant aspects anticipations of Christianity; in the relevant cases Christian expansion and revival were limited to those societies that preserved the indigenous name for God. It suggests that theologically God had preceded the missionary in Africa, a fact that Bible translation clinched with decisive authority.

QUESTION 15: With all that granted, would you say the growth and renewal in world Christianity have been all gain and no loss?

ANSWER: No, it's been a bit of both.

QUESTION 16: Can you say more?

ANSWER: Yes. On the gain side the churches have grown; membership has increased, in many cases exponentially; and communities of hope have come into being in areas of strife and despair. But on the loss side, false prophets have appeared, schisms have spread, the simple and ignorant have been taken advantage of, ethnic hostility has flared into grim killings, and ethical standards have slipped with political corruption. There has been structural collapse of the public order, but the dogma of secularization precludes a public role for religion even in this dire situation. Indeed, religion is held responsible for the failure.

QUESTION 17: I don't know if we should be enthusiastic about Christian expansion if this sad legacy is the result. But that's a statement. Here is the question: Should we be doing any rejoicing with such a mixed bag?

ANSWER: Well, we should not rejoice because utopia has arrived nor be afraid because Armageddon is threatened, but rather, we should take heart because suffering people have found faith and hope. The people who have lined up, determined to enter the church, have eaten of the bread of adversity and tasted the waters of affliction, and still they press to come into the church. The church exists to welcome precisely such as these, their personal or material circumstances notwithstanding. There is no entrance fee for membership because the kingdom of God is especially for the least among us. Who are we to begrudge them? Also, I don't want to paint too one-sided a picture, or even to suggest that joining the church solves all the problems of life and society.

QUESTION 18: What, then, are you suggesting?

ANSWER: I'm suggesting that for the new African Christians the church is a good place to work out the problems and challenges of life and society. The norms of faith and forgiveness, undergirded by the practice of the arts of charitable action, community solidarity, trust, and faithfulness, offer a way forward for all of society. The Christian example is part of the public good, not apart from it.

QUESTION 19: When you speak of the public good, don't you think it's harmful to talk of Christian expansion because of its sectarian, triumphalist overtones? Should we not instead be talking about goodwill among all people without regard to religious labels?

ANSWER: I see where you're headed. Yes, by all means let us talk about the expansion of goodwill among all people, but let us not make that goodwill an alternative or a rival to religion lest we become sectarian and triumphalist by another way.

QUESTION 20: Good move. But I still wonder whether we'd be better off without the Christian label in view of Christianity's lamentable record in slavery, racism, colonialism, and intolerance. Again that is a statement. But could you take it as a question? Should Christians not be spending their time in breast-beating rather than in gloating?

ANSWER: I support penance among Christians and oppose all gloating, it goes without saying, but I'm reluctant to accept the implicit thesis that Christian wrongdoing disqualifies all future conversions any more than Christian good deeds justify Christian boasting. I could put it in the form of a question: Why should Christianity not be absolved by the deeds of the saints of the church even as the deeds of sinners condemn it? But take that as a rhetorical question.

Continental Shift: Interpreting the Expansion

QUESTION 21: Let me press with a direct question. I will hold my personal objections in check for the time being. You said the evidence for the expansion of Christianity is little in doubt. Are you suggesting that the explanation and interpretation may be?

ANSWER: Yes, precisely.

QUESTION 22: How then do the explanation and interpretation differ from the evidence?

ANSWER: The explanation and interpretation of Christian expansion usually carry a great deal of the

Western guilt complex, and so deflect attention from the facts on the ground. I guess I would also maintain that the Western guilt complex hinders us from acknowledging the role of local agents in the story of the planting of the church in Africa. The West still looms so large in the standard accounts of Third World Christianity that there is little room for the men and women on the ground who were responsible for church planting.

QUESTION 23: But you probably mean something more by interpretation, don't you?

ANSWER: How perceptive. Yes, I do. People want to interpret Christianity by standards of exegesis and doctrine familiar to them, something that the Christendom model of the church warranted. World Christianity, by contrast, must be interpreted by a plurality of models of inculturation in line with the variety of local idioms and practices. The mental habits of Christendom predispose us to look for one essence of the faith, with a corresponding global political structure as safeguard, whereas world Christianity challenges us to pay attention to the dynamic power of the gospel and to the open-ended character of communities of faith. Doctrine and exegesis are important, it should be stressed, but not without the dimension of personal experience and the network of human interactions.

QUESTION 24: It's ironic that guilt over the wrongs the West committed in the field should perpetuate further wrongs against those still left in the field. Anyhow, my question is whether you think there can be a genuine convergence between a Christian Africa and a secular

West, given the lopsided nature of the strength of Christianity in the two societies.

ANSWER: That's a tough question, and I don't know the answer. Some writers say a major challenge is posed to Western civilization by the disconcerting fact that what were once its critical religious and moral convictions are now primarily upheld by communities belonging to a post-Western Christianity. In that view Christian militancy will rise to threaten the values of a liberal West. I personally don't see much evidence of such a global clash being fomented by a post-Western Christianity. Nor do I see a simple convergence resulting from a reevangelization of the West and a restoration of its critical religious heritage. At present one is struck by the disparity: Africa has become, or is becoming, a Christian continent in cultural as well as numerical terms, while on the same scale the West has become, or is rapidly becoming, a post-Christian society. Whether that will mean a corresponding estrangement in sympathy and outlook, I don't know. Maybe we should suspend the subject for now.

QUESTION 25: An arresting phrase, "Africa a Christian continent." It rings strange to Western ears. Would you expand on it? You mean more than statistical changes, don't you?

ANSWER: Yes, I do. True, the statistical weight has moved Africa firmly into the Christian orbit, and that happened only a few years ago, which is why the notion is so novel and so dramatic. But we should bear in mind that Christianity from its origin was marked by serial retreat and advance as an intercultural process. Bethlehem and Jerusalem were superseded by Antioch and Athens, while Egypt and Carthage soon gave place to Rome. Rival centers multiplied the chances of further contraction and expansion. Then it was the turn of the North Atlantic to inherit the mantle before the next momentous phase brought the religion to the Southern Hemisphere, with Africa representing the most recent continental shift. These developments went beyond merely adding more names to the books; they had to do with cultural shifts, with changing the books themselves. This serial feature of the history of Christianity is largely hidden from people in the West now living in a post-Christian culture. Even in Africa itself the churches were caught unprepared, and are scarcely able to cope with the elementary issue of absorbing new members, let alone with the deeper issues of formation and training.

QUESTION 26: So the expansion is not an unmitigated success story for the churches either?

ANSWER: No, expansion creates problems of scale and timing. The end of the colonial era was also the end of the missionary era. At the time the verdict on a century of missionary labor by common consent was all toil and little gain. When subsequently large hauls of converts started arriving in the church, there was consternation. Had not the emissaries from the West labored through long nights and taken little? What could prepare their otherwise poorly equipped local successors for the new burst of life? There was astonished disbelief, you can well understand.

QUESTION 27: Many people in the West are skeptical

that Christianity has done much good in Africa, or anywhere else for that matter. They think of what white rule
has done in Zimbabwe or Rhodesia; the effects in Kenya
of the white emergency rule in the 1950s; the results in
South Africa of a Calvinist-inspired apartheid regime; of
the ethnic killings in Rwanda and Burundi; and now of
an AIDS epidemic in which over 4,900 people die daily.
Where is the good news in that?

ANSWER: There's not much, I agree. I should stress,
however, that perhaps because of such crises and the related search for healing and wholeness, Christianity has
remained a potent force in the lives of Africans, and the
churches as major social institutions have an effect far
out of proportion to the resources they command. It is as
social institutions that they have been involved in the
AIDS crisis, in mediation efforts in Rwanda and Burundi, in efforts in community building, in education, in
the advancement of women, in peace and justice projects. As for apartheid, African Christian leaders took a
prominent part in challenging white supremacist power
and in working for truth, forgiveness, and reconciliation.

But I cannot leave the subject there without making a
comparison with the West itself. After all, the two devas-
tating world wars of the twentieth century, 1914 and 1939,
wars that engulfed the rest of the world, were led by the
Christian countries of Europe. My grandmother's only
son, Mamadi Sidibe, was killed in one of those wars fight-
ing as a British-conscripted soldier. His widow was never
told of his death, and her surviving daughter, my cousin,
still lives in penury. Furthermore, Christianity did not

prevent the cold war and the nuclear proliferation that came with it. I don't know what conclusion we should draw from this except to say that the story of Christianity is still unfolding, is still cutting for itself fresh channels in Africa. We do not yet know how that story will end. All we know is that many more are yet to join that story. And there is as yet little evidence that Christian Africa will repeat the disasters of Christian Europe.

Let me, if you will allow, assess the issue in this way. African Christianity has not been a bitterly fought religion: there have been no ecclesiastical courts condemning unbelievers, heretics, and witches to death; no bloody battles of doctrine and polity; no territorial aggrandizement by churches; no jihads against infidels; no fatwas against women; no amputations, lynchings, ostracism, penalties, or public condemnations of doctrinal difference or dissent. The lines of Christian profession have not been etched in the blood of enemies. To that extent, at least African Christianity has diverged strikingly from sixteenth- and seventeenth-century Christendom.

QUESTION 28: That may well be, but don't you have denominationalism in Africa?

ANSWER: Yes and no! If by denominationalism you mean a proliferation of different churches and the sects they spawn, Africa is up to its ears in the stuff. And besides, many of these groups are transplants from Europe and North America. Africa adds its own brand names to the mix, more than seventy times seven. If, on the other hand, by denominationalism you mean the ideology of intolerance, exclusivism, social stratification, and class separation, then the answer is no. You will find members of the respectable, governing classes as well as the poor randomly scattered among all the major churches and denominations. The lines separating the denominations are often links rather than barriers, especially since Vatican II, but they were often that even before it.

Models of Faith and Community

QUESTION 29: Would you allow the impression to be created that African Christianity has no major theological or polity problems to resolve, and that mass excitement can substitute for membership, identity, and sustained understanding?

ANSWER: No, because I think that would be inaccurate. The expansion of Christianity has thrown up numerous knotty problems of apostolic polity and religious interpretation, yet so recent was the expansion that the churches are still in the early stages of stocktaking. Fishing nets in the form of religious vocations, formation, and apostolic structures will be needed to avert disarray and disenchantment. Excitement alone cannot suffice for apostolic obedience. But notice that it is the momentum of the expansion that has induced the stocktaking. Growth requires the expansion of both physical buildings and horizons to make room for new models of truth and community.

QUESTION 30: If we may return to the statistics of African Christian expansion — you gave a lot of facts and figures, and went over them too quickly. You suggested that more people converted to Christianity since the end of colonial rule than in the entire period of the colonial empires. Many people in the West find that hard to understand. How can Africans be Christian before they have been civilized? And how can they be civilized unless European rule has done that? I realize these are a lot of questions, but you understand what I'm getting at. Could you indicate what is happening today? Has the pace slowed down?

ANSWER: Well, yes, I see what you're getting at. But let me answer only the question about growth and its pace. The pace has not slowed down. In 1970 there were 120 million Christians, estimated; in 1998 the figure jumped to just under 330 million; and in 2000 to 350 million. The projections call for over 600 million Christians in twenty-five years. If those projections are right — and I will not go to the scaffold for them — apart from South America, Africa will have more Christians than any other continent, and that for the first time.

Conversion, Syncretism, and Cross-Cultural Horizons

QUESTION 31: Again, as I remarked earlier, that is unbelievable. What is fueling this extraordinary explosion?

ANSWER: I mentioned several factors earlier: the end of colonial rule; the effects of mother tongue development and Bible translation; indigenous cultural renewal and local agency; and the theological stimulation of the Christian adoption of the African names of God. A Western audience would be more convinced by economic and political reasons: the appeal of the West, the search for security, the need for foreign assistance, the power of international links and affiliation, and disenchantment with institutional and structural collapse in Africa. But this Western account of the phenomenon leaves open the question of what is cause and what consequence. It's like trying to separate wind and trees: Did the tempest of economic and political upheaval toss the conversions, or, which is more likely, have the conversions only demonstrated the limited relevance of economic and political dissruption? Maybe God has something to do with it, after all.

QUESTION 32: I can see how Western explanations after the fact are unsatisfactory. For one thing, they take little account of historical facts or of deliberate local agency. But even granting your premise of indigenous reasons for Christian expansion, are you saying Christianity was only a matter of cultural convenience, that Africans embraced the religion because it looked pretty much like one of their old cults?

ANSWER: Yes and no! People receive new ideas only in terms of the ideas they already have, and so, yes, Africans embraced Christianity because it resonated so well with the values of the old religions. "Mary Had a Little Lamb" might strike a chord beyond mere recreational diversion because, translated into the sensibilities of the native rhythm, it evokes dormant memories of the maiden as guardian spirit of the flocks once celebrated in the old village nursery rhymes. But, *no*, if by cultural convenience you mean a religion that makes no demands on the affections, loyalties, attitudes, and behavior of people. The old religions provided the rules, rewarding good conduct and punishing wrong, but they had only a limited ethical range: the family, the clan, the village, the tribe. Small-scale societies insulated people from historical pressures and thus removed the need for adjustments in people's worldview. Christianity answered this historical challenge by a reorientation of the worldview so that the old moral framework was reconfigured without being overthrown. It was not that the old spells, turning benign from overuse, had dulled the appetite, but that, under challenge, their spent potency sparked a clamor for a valiant God. People sensed in their hearts that Jesus did not mock their respect for the sacred or their clamor for an invincible Savior, and so they beat their sacred drums for him until the stars skipped and danced in the skies. After that dance the stars weren't little anymore. Christianity helped Africans to become renewed Africans, not remade Europeans.

QUESTION 33: Well, okay, that stands to reason. But here is the issue: Can you then say precisely and succinctly what conversion is?

ANSWER: Conversion is the turning of ourselves to God, and that means all of ourselves without leaving anything behind or outside. But that also means not replacing what is there with something else. Conversion is a refocusing of the mental life and its cultural/social underpinning and of our feelings, affections, and instincts, in the light of what God has done in Jesus. That is the most succinct and precise way I can think of defining the term.

QUESTION 34: How do you distinguish that from syncretism?

ANSWER: I distinguish it by appealing to the process whereby the Christian message is appropriated into existing local frameworks but still remains recognizably Christian, much like what the Greeks in places like Alexandria, Antioch, Athens, and Ephesus did with the Jewish heritage of Jesus. Syncretism represents the unresolved, unassimilated, and tension-filled mixing of Christian ideas with local custom and ritual, and that scarcely results in the kind of fulfilling change signaled by conversion and church membership. Besides, syncretism is the term we use for the religion of those we don't like. No one calls himself or herself a syncretist! It's a name we use of others, and not in a complimentary way. Unless we use the term as a judgment against our own forms of religious practice, I suggest we drop it altogether.

QUESTION 35: I just want to be clear on your meaning — conversion, you say, is fundamentally an internal process, not an externally imposed act, and converts are the ones who can best represent themselves before God without aid of foreign sponsors. Is that correct?

ANSWER: Yes.

QUESTION 36: But isn't that individualism run amok?

ANSWER: No. It is cultural and personal integrity grounded in solidarity with God and with the people of God.

QUESTION 37: But surely the individual is the one who converts, for you cannot convert by proxy, can you? Conversion is not filling a culture with extraneous material, is it?

ANSWER: No, it's not. But the individual doesn't convert to himself or herself. She converts to God as a social act — identifying herself with a distinctive community of faith and with others called to the life of faith. The individual act of conversion is not a rejection of community but the occasion for community.

QUESTION 38: How can we be sure people understand what they are converting to?

ANSWER: By the response of faith they freely make.

QUESTION 39: But shouldn't we be able to judge that response to see if it is real?

ANSWER: I can best answer that by asking a rhetorical question: How can we probe other people's interior motives without violating their integrity as moral agents? If we don't accept the right of people to act freely in what concerns their ultimate destiny, then haven't we violated the most basic principle of their dignity as human beings and as children of God? I think deciding on our own who is and is not a believer reduces religion to personal preference, and religion of that type is but a specimen of strident individualism. If you reject a person's understanding of himself or herself as religious, where would you stop? If you insist that you are entitled to your own con-

viction for or against religion but that others have no
such right, then haven't you denied them the freedom
you allowed yourself? It's hard to do that in good conscience, is it not? Belief premised on persuasion fosters
the spirit of freedom and tolerance, while suppression, or
imposition, of belief suffocates the spirit. That's why the
church teaches conversion on the grounds that no one
can be saved against his or her will. Conversion makes
the means of personal persuasion consonant with the
end of personal integrity.

QUESTION 40: With respect, I disagree. I think if we
say religion is whatever people say it is, the confusion
from conflicting claims about religion would reduce it to
a meaningless jumble, with inchoate bits and pieces of it
scattered unclaimed among various domains of human
endeavor. Surely, for religion to have any sort of name or
identity, you have to draw the line somewhere, don't you?

ANSWER: Yes, for religion to have an identity, you do
have to draw the line somewhere, but I would be reluctant to draw it so inflexibly as to intrude on the sovereign
claim of conscience. That does not, however, rule out the
need for structures of proclamation, instruction,
apologetics, and the other ways by which a faith tradition
promotes and sustains itself. So, in direct answer to your
question about drawing a line, I would say how a faith
commitment is recognized has to do with matters of
identity and boundary. It's not just one person saying he
or she is a Christian that makes a faith tradition, but the
community in which such a faith profession has the potential to flourish. Draw a line, then, if you must, but let

it be a line that connects, grows, and expands. Let it be a living line.

Religion and the Individual: Philosophical Undercurrents

QUESTION 41: I'm sorry, I can't leave the subject there. If we grant that conversion is to God, how can the native mind comprehend such a lofty idea at all without proper tutoring?

ANSWER: Reliable witnesses have reported that at the heart of ethnic religious experience stands a creative power with a name and function, in fact with many names and functions. Such reporting is simultaneous with the earliest evidence. As a pagan elder assured an experienced colonial administrator, "God and Jesus do not belong only to the Protestants and Roman Catholics. They belong to pagans also. [God and Jesus] are not surrounded by a fence up there in Heaven, and we do not have to run into a mission fence to find them here on earth. They are everywhere, like Auriaria and Tabuariki and Tituaabine. We can take them for our own friends if we want them. And some of them did precisely that, by the simple expedient of using the names of power in their magic of kindness."[6] No missionary tutoring was necessary to establish the idea of a personal God.

6. Arthur Grimble, *A Pattern of Islands* (London: John Murray, 1960), 120.

QUESTION 42: But isn't it a fact that primitive people thought of God as trees, animals, nature, superhuman agents, and anything else that awed or bamboozled them? Isn't that how an elevated monotheism evolved in stages from the downward spiral of superstitious polytheism? It would make sense, wouldn't it, to think of Africans being lifted in stages from enslavement to nature's fickle moods and the delusory idea of many gods, to the refined philosophical ideal of one God in line with the improvements in their material circumstances? As bush tracks fade away to make room for roads and highways, the tribe gradually dissolves into individual wage earners able to support their families. The children of these wage earners, growing up in new sprawling townships, sidestep initiation rites and other village rites of passage and enroll in school where they join children from other tribes. After learning to read, these children become numbered and salaried employees and, with a mailing address, turn into captured subjects of the state. They are then able to move upscale from round huts and floor mats to square houses and frame beds. The new medium of communication is a European language, the only language the children had in common at school. That language, as the language of history, geography, mathematics, and science, gives access to the world of rational thought and self-knowledge, and becomes the vehicle by which the circle of local deities and their tribal-size universe is ruptured to reveal an unprecedented cosmopolitan and an ethnically untainted worldview. The rainbow is God's smile until seen through Newton's prism. Isn't that how tribal religions evolved?

ANSWER: You express yourself eloquently. But the whole debate about evolution in religion has not, unfortunately, been as productive as writers such as Robertson Smith, Sigmund Freud, Lévy-Bruhl, Edward Tylor, Durkheim, and Herbert Spencer once thought, and so I'm not sure it's helpful to return to it now, unless you insist. From the historical evidence, however, an indubitable picture emerges of one God who is set before the so-called tribesman like a transcendent presence who is personal and who is prior (compare, for instance, the views of Wilhelm Schmidt and Hermann Baumann). That conflicts with the notion of African religions as naturalistic projections. It was Sir James Frazer, no less, who affirmed: "The mind of man refuses to acquiesce in the phenomena of sense."

QUESTION 43: I'm not ready to give up. God as a philosophical ideal is uncreated, infinite, without form, and inaccessible. The African tribesman, by contrast, is so constrained by the unpredictable shortness of life, and by its cruelty and privations while it lasts, that he cannot accede to any rational notion of a reality beyond this life. His infantile need for parental security still unsatiated, he fantasizes that into an all-indulging mumbo jumbo. His mind is so fettered by his fears and his simple needs, so steeped in a charmed circle of self-fulfilling justifications, that it is not free for the task of critical self-reflection, is it? Isn't that why the tribes fixated on nature as their enchanted master, believing that what you call a living line connects them to the phenomena of nature? "Twinkle, twinkle, little stars" became winking little divinities in the sky. The tribesman takes a false step from *nomina* to *numina,* from chance to cause, perception to concept, and so engages in a procedure that shows logical immaturity. It shows the tribesman a prisoner of his thoughts, trapped in the oscillation of nature, in turn teasing with its thrills and tormenting with its terrors. As the popular hymn says, "The heathen in his blindness bows to wood and stone." These views, needless to say, are based on generally accepted objective criteria drawn from studies about the development of mental life.[7] In the circumstances, why should the high-minded God of Christianity, refined by centuries of sustained intellectual endeavor as a mental construct, have anything to say to an illiterate culture? And doesn't that place individual acts of conversion on a bank of sand?

ANSWER: You are provocative, and so let me oblige. Heathens come in many hues, it seems, for another hymn (by Kipling) has different ones in mind when it says, "For heathen heart that puts her trust / In reeking tube and iron shard," referring to Europeans. Your argument can just as easily be applied to the make-believe world of Hollywood, where sophisticated people seem in turn to acquiesce in the phenomena of sense by just as gullibly constructing their picture of the world from the fantasy images of the screen, with heroes and heroines, the glitzy mumbos and jumbos of sense impression, leaping from the screen to godlike veneration in real life.

7. See Sir Karl Popper, *The Open Society and Its Enemies,* 2 vols. (London, 1966).

In this make-believe world, virtual reality casts a spell on real world experience, with life imitating art. Movies and television have the power to make people feel possessed. The "tribesman," then, is no different, if that is your point. Which leaves you pondering what, if anything, has changed about perception in the transition to modern culture, which is the most visual of cultures.

As to your claims about objectivity, I should be more modest there, because I don't know what is objective about making assertions about other cultures based on the certainties of your own. Once you exclude societies other than the West from what you call "generally accepted objective criteria," then you place the "general" on no more a secure foundation than conversion.

In any case, not to lose the thread of your argument, it seems to me you're asking the same question in different ways. Let me try to advance the discussion by explaining that evolution at first misled us about the evidence of religious practice in African societies, predisposing us to look for a phased transition from baseline polytheism to a successive elevated monotheism. We failed to realize, however, that the same Africans who thought of and worshiped God as one also maintained devotion to the lesser deities as divine hypostases, as the refractions and manifestations of God. It was not a case of either/or, but of the one God having many attributes — much in line, in fact, with Old Testament ideas and practice.[8]

8. Aubrey R. Johnson, *The One and the Many in the Israelite Conception of God* (Cardiff: University of Wales Press, 1961).

QUESTION 44: A picture, they say, is worth a thousand words. A well-chosen example can make a point more vividly than can general theory, for which theology, I am sorry to say, has a particular weakness. Theologians shelter in droves behind the Chinese Wall of antiquarian abstraction, with a refined interest in theory rather than engagement with real religious people. At any rate, can you give some concrete examples of the kind of theological thinking you say happens among tribal people?

ANSWER: Yes, I can. By the way, your point is well taken about theology having a blind spot for dynamic images in spite of their prevalence in religion. We have one striking example of articulate, precise theological reflection on God by a tribal people who, otherwise cribbed and confined by nature, might be deemed incapable of conceptualizing God at all. They lack a tradition of political centralization and commensurate economic organization that Europeans regard as the basis of rational thought. This is the widely quoted *confessio fidei* of the Pygmies of the Congo. Nothing in their culture or in their limited and deprived physical circumstances prepares us for the incisive insight of these words:

> In the beginning was God,
> Today is God,
> Tomorrow will be God.
> Who can make an image of God?
> He has no body.
> He is a word that comes out of your mouth.
> That word! It is no more,

It is past, and still it lives!
So is God.

As the Herero of Namibia put it, God, called by them
Ndjambi Karunga, is the one who owns the sky, and is not
in the graves, a God of blessing who is angry with nobody
and punishes nobody. In this worldview human beings
are constituted of the moral and social, and so it behooves
them to remember God in their doings and relationships.
A tribe, accordingly, assures its members: death does not
come to someone for whom prayer is made; rather, death
comes to those who trust in their own strength, who trust
in "reeking tube and iron shard." This is a far cry from the
gnostic assertion of Alfred North Whitehead that religion
is what individuals do with their own solitariness.[9] In the
psychological view religion has its source in man's own
nature; in the sociological view it lies in man's place in society and the world; while in the anthropological view it
lies in the myth of primitive man. In effect, religion is an
illusion, destined to dissipate with advances in reason and
material improvement.

If you remember, I said earlier that conversion was to
God; I did not say it was to European or other people's
theories of God. I accept that conversion puts the gospel
through the crucible of its host culture, but Europe is not
host to Africa in the things of God, do you think? The
gospel is not a creed for race delinquency.

9. Alfred North Whitehead, *Religion in the Making* (Cambridge,
1927), 6.

QUESTION 45: Almost thou persuadest me, as the wizened potentate said, acknowledging the apostle's eloquence (Acts 26:28). You certainly have my attention, but I still have a flea in my ear. Here's why. Native populations were so mesmerized by the material wealth of Europeans that they sublimated their aroused desire for European goods into a picture of heaven. Eternal bliss consisted of well-fed, smartly attired, cosseted people lounging in easy chairs or being chauffeured around in limousines and puffing away on their cigars, a lifelike image of Europeans and their inventions that fastened itself on the native imagination to tickle the fancy of infantile obsession. Thus two or three Europeans were enough to make a dream team. A facile Christianity was accordingly projected into a cargo cult to feed the shallow appetite for religion. Doesn't that undercut your claim about the so-called indigenous theological advantage?

ANSWER: I'm not sure it does. Cargo cults were also a potent force of resistance to European intrusion on local societies. Besides, not all primal religions were cargo cults, and not all cargo cults were friendly to Christianity. Those that were had their worldly outlook profoundly changed from the encounter. Struggle and suspicion, rather than material or wish fulfillment, marked the path to conversion and to critical self-orientation. So I will still make my pitch for the indigenous theological advantage, especially with the impact of Bible translation.

Indigenous Discovery

QUESTION 46: I want to move the discussion to another issue and ask which, in your view, is the more helpful way of describing the process: As the Christian discovery of indigenous societies or the indigenous discovery of Christianity? What's at stake in the distinction?

ANSWER: The Christian discovery of indigenous societies describes the process of missionaries from the West coming to Africa or Asia and converting people, often with political incentives and material inducements. The indigenous discovery of Christianity, by contrast, describes local people encountering the religion through mother tongue discernment and in the light of the people's own needs and experiences. The indigenous discovery places the emphasis on unintended local consequences, leaving the way open for indigenous agency and leadership, while the Christian discovery looks to the originating impulses and the Western cultural binding of religion. The one stresses external transmission, and the other internal appropriation.

QUESTION 47: Are you suggesting Christianity should be reinvented, and that faith should be a genealogical unit of tribal value, what is euphemistically referred to as ancestor worship?

ANSWER: That's a fair question. For people converting to Christianity in a culture previously unevangelized, yes, there is a begin-again quality to religious experience. But this is not so much reinvention as conversion, with the convert a fresh impression of faith encounter. Christianity is not a garment made to specifications of a bygone golden age, nor is it an add-on whimsical patchwork rigged up without regard to the overall design. Rather, Christianity is a multicolored fabric where each new thread, chosen and refined at the Designer's hand, adds luster and strength to the whole. In this pattern of faith affirmation we should stress the importance of interwoven solidarity with fellow believers, past, present, and future.

QUESTION 48: You have more to say, surely. Does not the call to faith make reasonable the refusal of faith, so that the invitation to faith may gratuitously center attention on strategy, whether successful or not, rather than on God as faith's object? And doesn't that introduce into your fabric a shred of human ambiguity, a tangled line that snags the pattern?

ANSWER: Faith is not a demilitarized zone, if I may shift figures. It is life's battlefront of encounter, risk, struggle, suffering, choice, grace, and deliverance. It is therefore not fatal to faith that people choose and decide freely, however great the risk of human entanglement; otherwise faith would cease to be what it is. No one can be saved against his or her will, though the will, prone to willfulness, is not an end in itself. Conversion is not to people, to techniques, or even to theories, but to God in whom is our true freedom, and the proof of that is in the knowledge and love God grants. Knowledge of God's gracious gift is assured only by God, and by means of others that God may choose. Admittedly, our knowledge of

God's assurance, marked by struggle and suffering, varies, but God granted us that knowledge, such as it is, and with it grace so that even our imperfect knowledge may not condemn us. The fact of God knowing us becomes personal when we consent to be so known. That way we attain to our deepest humanity from the fact of God having inbreathed us. That's what faith and conversion are all about.

Reason, Custom, Commitment, and Human Solidarity

QUESTION 49: I want to understand from this theological account you are giving that implicit in it is the idea that Europeans have something to learn about Christianity and about themselves from Africa's recent theological encounter with Christianity. Is that what you think?

ANSWER: Yes.

QUESTION 50: Can you say what that is in light of your statement about conversion to God rather than to other people's notions of God (#44 above)? Theology is not just about arithmetic in the pew, nor for that matter, if I may anticipate the subject, is Bible translation a crash course in head-hunting, is it?

ANSWER: No, theology is not, nor is Bible translation, but religion is not about deserted pews, either. Theology's cross-border promises are greater than the boundary-fixed rule for it as a domesticated activity of the mind. Theology cannot go on subsisting on the legacy of rented pews. As I explained in my introductory comments, in Bible translation the local names for God were adopted as the personal God of Scripture, laying the basis for eventual large-scale conversion and renewal. Europeans can gain a lot of insight from that theological transposition. Second, the West can learn from the fact that the gospel entered a particularly promising historical phase of cultural transformation when in the nineteenth and twentieth centuries it encountered the religions and societies of Africa, all that with little trace of the pessimistic prognosis evolution decreed for it (#42, 43 above). I just don't see how Europeans can continue — and I devoutly hope they do continue — to study and teach Christianity without paying heed to examples of Christianity's successful cross-border expansion in postcolonial societies. Christianity is a world religion of recent vintage with energy to renew the church as it reels exhausted from its pact with secularism.

QUESTION 51: But the bulk of the theological literature continues to be produced in the West, indicating that the West still enjoys intellectual advantage in Christianity. Given that, can you think of why there might be wider benefits for the church in what is happening in Christian Africa?

ANSWER: There must be wider benefits for all in the movements of renewal taking place in a post-Western world Christianity. The tradition of exegesis that has been practiced in the West seems to have run its course. There are too many instances of recycling and cultural discounting, and too willing a tendency to suppress difference, for us not to think that the envelope can't be pushed much further. The standard exegesis spins faith into just more cultural filibuster. Yet in Africa and elsewhere there is enough sense of commodiousness, with fresh materials being introduced into Scripture, prayers, hymns, and liturgy, for that not to affect how people in the West think and speak about the gospel and the church. In Nigeria, Yoruba converts to Christianity, for example, have the rich heritage of Ifa divination to draw upon as they try to express their newfound faith in the terms the Yoruba idiom makes natural for them. The name for savior, *Olugbala,* for instance, is preloaded with older Yoruba theological notions of divine power, solicitude, and redemptive suffering. *Olugbala* accedes to the Jesus of Scripture without dumping the old cargo.

The Maasai of East Africa, to take another example, speak in their so-named African Creed of believing as a community rather than as individuals, and instead of casting their creed in cognitive abstract terms of the seen and unseen, of Christ as eternally begotten of the Father, God from God, light from light, begotten not made, etc., they speak of a journey of faith in a God who out of love created the world and us, of how they once knew the High God in darkness but now know this God in the light. The creed continues with God's promises in Scripture and momentously in Jesus, "a man in the flesh, a Jew by tribe, born poor in a little village, who left his home and was always on safari doing good, curing people by the power of God," until finally he was rejected by his people, tortured and nailed, hands and feet, to a cross, and died. Then the irony of the historical Jesus is clinched with a stunning understatement with the words, "He lay buried in the grave, but the hyenas did not touch him, and on the third day he rose from the grave." A note of eschatological joy and hope swells to conclude the creed: "We are waiting for Him [Jesus]. He is alive. He lives. This we believe. Amen." The Jesus of the African Creed is a solid historical figure, steeped in his Jewish culture, swept up in the controversies of the day, put to death without being shamed, witnessed to by Scripture, anointed and abiding through the Holy Spirit, a channel of God's grace, and present in the world through sacrament, mission, and service to one another.

There is little sign in the creed, as there is in the Nicene Creed, of the words smelling of the litigious lamp, of the scars of bitter theological battle, of rubbing in the noses of the vanquished, of haunting heresy, or of the West's twilight mood. Maasai ideas of God are not as prickly, and it is as such that they have shaped the outlook of their African Creed. Such evidence is assurance, too, that the indigenization and inculturation of the gospel stand to benefit the wider church.

QUESTION 52: Point well taken. But aren't you still underestimating Europe's intellectual and material superiority, and the unifying ideology of preeminence all that breeds? For example, are you implying, as you seemed to earlier, that religious loyalty is something real and genuine and not dependent on political affiliation or economic advantage, that converts may be conservative or radical theologically without necessarily lining up with corresponding political alignments in the West?

ANSWER: Yes, I am. Not to contradict you, but I should say that Europe's power makes it answerable for what it does or doesn't do. The picture about political affiliation may, however, be complicated by liberation theologians aligning themselves with progressive groups in the West, but most ordinary Christian converts would have no such formal links. You get a sense of this, I think, in African American Christianity's separateness from American evangelical as well as American mainline Protestantism. Even a preeminent unifying ideology seems incapable of defying difference.

QUESTION 53: So let me go back to my question (#24 above) about the convergence or disparity between a Christian but still underdeveloped Africa and an advanced secular West. You said then it was a tough question and you pleaded ignorance. But if your answer is correct about Christianity not being determined and produced by unifying economic and political forces, that suggests a major divergence with Western explanations in terms of the primacy of material motivation in religious belief. It is an accepted rule in the West that religion may be allowed within the bounds of reason alone, and so revelation, miracle stories, and notions of the supernatural must be sifted to mesh with the refined rules of reason. So, yes, Europeans tolerate religion as one of the social indiscretions, and if they have to, take it with a rational pinch of salt. Accordingly they read the Bible with a specially designed minimalist tool to remove the

naive sediment of pious myth. Only the skill in disman-
tling the Bible as mythology makes it worth our attention
at all. Doesn't that preclude a convergence between Africa and the West?

ANSWER: If we take a narrow view of the West in its
flag-flapping Enlightenment bluster, yes, a convergence
would be hard to envisage, and would in any case be
moot. Still, I'm not sure that with its dogma of reason the
West is fully protected. To amend George Herbert, society first seasons its children at home, then gives them
over to schoolmasters who deliver them bound to rules of
reason, holding them in nets and stratagems of dispas-
sionate logic before the whole fine array is blown away
with one cunning secret sin ("one cunning bosome
sinne"). In any case, you will notice that I began with the
concrete facts of the case for world Christianity, not with
a general philosophy of religion. The practices religious
people have engaged in on the ground could yield insight
no less penetrating than disciplined philosophical reflection. But your point is well taken. The West, viewed
broadly as a cultural system of ethics, images, music, literature as well as science and technology, has reduced
the mystery of God to a cultural filibuster. Truth cannot
be known with certainty, and one can be certain about
that, and about the related confident cultural relativism
that postpones indefinitely questions of finality. So a
gnostic religious faith continues to be widespread in the
West in spite of demands for the primacy of reason. It
suggests antagonism, not to faith as such, but to institutional religion. Yet what is religion without form? The

scruples of the West notwithstanding, the churches have continued to grow beyond the West on the basis of their strong evangelical emphasis. It turns out that colonial rule as the frame of Christianity's civilizing mission has been superseded by the onward march of the religion. If we recall Muslim progress in the same period, we could say that for religion in general colonialism and civilization were not indispensable, however fortuitous the conjunction with religion might be.

For its part, academic theology, understood as the Western intellectual system of religious thought, came into play only after the expansion, if even then. In the event, the church has continued to expand in Africa, and the West has interacted with Africa and the rest of the Third World on the basis not only of economic superiority but also of human rights, justice, fairer distribution of wealth, and the global demographic movement of people. Economic partnership in such a world, South Africa's Thabo Mbeki argued, should foster renewed interest in our common humanity as the foundation of global relations.[10] Chinua Achebe expressed a similar idea when he told a meeting of the Organization for Economic Cooperation and Development that "Africa is people," not just units, numbers, trends, and scale. The West, too, cannot live by bread, or by reason, alone. Besides, it is easy to halve the potato where there is understanding. We may thus indulge a modest hope for a meeting of minds.

10. Thabo Mbeki, "Africa's New Realism," *New York Times*, June 24, 2002, op-ed page.

A word or two more about the human side of global encounter. Because of its wealth and influence, the United States has attracted to its shores people from many different parts of the world with different backgrounds, and among them has been a sizable number of foreign students who have been welcomed into American homes as guests and who have made deep and lasting friendships as a result of such experiences. The subtle effects of these cross-cultural friendships will undoubtedly take time to work through the structures and institutions, but in the long term they are destined to influence the nature and character of international relations. Human bonds are intangibles that are hard to measure, admittedly, but they are no less profound in their influence.

QUESTION 54: Do you have any specific examples in mind?

ANSWER: Take a random example that involves the Maasai. News of the terrorist attacks on September 11, 2001, did not reach the tribe until a Maasai student returned from the United States to his people with the story some eight months after the fact. Using Maasai narrative form, the student carefully recounted the scale and details of the attacks, including people jumping from windows to escape the fires, and the thousands who perished. This so moved the Maasai that they staged a solemn ceremony in an open field where they blessed fourteen cows as a gift in sympathy to the people of the United States, pledging with their bows and arrows to hunt down the terrorists in question. A bemused senior

U.S. embassy official in Nairobi made the trek through the bush to receive the cows.[11] The heart, the sages say, is the toughest part of the body. Tenderness is in the hands. A public acknowledgment of the gift was subsequently broadcast on National Public Radio (June 8, 2002). It spoke of the gratitude of the American people for the generosity and thoughtfulness of the Maasai. You cannot put a price on such gestures of hands extended in friendship, nor count in number their interpersonal effect.

Problem of Ideology

QUESTION 55: That's very interesting, but I'm not done yet. I asked you before (#30 above) how the natives could become Christian without having been civilized at the hands of Europeans. Conversion requires civilization, something that the ideology of empire provides. Remember the famous slogan about the Bible and plow combining to save Africa for commerce, civilization, and Christianity, the three Cs? Would you then answer my point about a progressive ideology? You haven't responded to that issue, have you?

ANSWER: No, I haven't; so let me do so now. Ideologies, as I understand them, do not just fade away to indulge a world open to new experiences and wider sympathies. Ideologies are mental canopies that set the horizons

---

11. "Where 9/11 News Is Late, but Aid Is Swift," *New York Times,* June 3, 2002, p. 1.

of what is acceptable in the world of ideas and values, and that do not allow circumstances to question their own value. Slavery, for example, relied on an ideology well expressed by an eighteenth-century officer of the Crown: "We shall take things as they are, and reason from them in their present state, and not from that wherein we could hope them to be. We cannot think of giving up the slave trade." Ideologies thus offer leak-proof protection against uncertainty and reciprocity, and the notion of the world as "constructed" or "imagined" helps to seal that protection. It's a linear, uncomplicated universe, illuminated by only one shaft of light: first do to others what they are not allowed to do to you. That is why I have not felt it productive to respond to triumphalist slogans of superior Western agency, or to strident claims of Third World victimization, for that matter. Instead, I have wanted to tell the story about a phase of world history beyond the West that at present has lacked an ideology of appeal. I want to shift attitudes, and once that happens, the evidence that now exists in such abundance can at last receive its long-overdue recognition. The study and teaching of religion and culture broadly conceived would thereby be enriched. That means, however, a willingness not to forgo ideology entirely, but to relent a little on it.

Impetus in the Old Order: China's Response

QUESTION 56: I can see the merit of not getting too distracted by the West's cultural controversies, and so should get on with the matter at hand. Where else, besides Africa, do you see a potential for Christian expansion?

ANSWER: I think mainland China is poised for a major development, perhaps only years away.

QUESTION 57: Why do you think that?

ANSWER: Because of reports I read of growing interest in Christianity, and of government attentiveness to the subject. The Chinese seem to reason — whether rightly or not is not for us to say — that Christianity might be the clue to the apparent success and dynamism of the West and might offer them a similar advantage if they understood it.

QUESTION 58: But why should a great and ancient civilization like China not find the resources it needs from its own vast intellectual reserves?

ANSWER: Perhaps it can and perhaps it should. After the upheavals of the Cultural Revolution of the 1960s, however, confidence in the old codes was profoundly shaken, and the rebuilding that was undertaken subsequently prompted new intellectual questions. The Cultural Revolution destroyed the values of the ancient code of filial piety. The old masters appeared too tame, and the new youth too restless to accede to the commands of their leaders. Confucian ethics was structurally too deeply invested in the mandate of heaven to keep pace with the needs of a dynamic society eager for a role in the modern world. Buddhism for the same reason was perceived as lacking in the critical historical consciousness and activist drive the new China needed in a competitive global world. Similarly, messianic Marxism, though awash in revolutionary activism, represented still an inflexible ideology of power and control too wrenching to offer any assurance and guidance about how China's classical past might find fulfillment in new times.

In addition to taking a new interest in Christianity, China has been sending out graduate students to study in the West. China's current leaders have also seized the initiative and called for a major overhaul of the government's ideological superstructure. President Jiang Zemin, for example, has called for a campaign entitled "Three Represents," meaning the Communist Party should no longer just represent workers but should represent "advanced productive forces, advanced Chinese culture and the fundamental interests of the majority."[12] According to reports, even Mao recognized that religion was a vital subject in the emerging China of the 1960s. The Chinese seem more willing now than they have been to allow circumstances to affect ideology, rather than the other way round. All these things seem to me straws in the wind. People are ready and eager for change, and so they look to Christianity, and to the immense Jewish heritage undergirding it, for direction. Who knows the long-term outcome of this new phase in China's long and distinguished history?

QUESTION 59: China is so different from the West. Why should Christianity as a Western religion be compatible with its very different context?

---

12. "China's Communists Try to Decide What They Stand For," *New York Times,* May 1, 2002, p. A3.

ANSWER: Perhaps because Christianity is no longer "Christendom," a religion of one cultural mandate. We would do well to remember that the language of Christianity is the language of the people, whoever they happen to be. The Chinese, therefore, do not have to renounce their language or their culture to embrace Christianity. We should learn by now that the gospel is not the monopoly of the West, as African Christianity has demonstrated.

QUESTION 60: So what you're saying is that Christianity belongs to all cultures. That's news for many in the West. People will stop their ears to that.

ANSWER: That's what I'm saying.

QUESTION 61: Why, then, did Christianity suppress so many native cultures? Why is the religion so intolerant of pluralism and multiculturalism?

ANSWER: I'm not ducking your question when I say that Christianity is the religion of over two thousand different language groups in the world. More people pray and worship in more languages in Christianity than in any other religion in the world. Furthermore, Christianity has been the impulse behind the creation of more dictionaries and grammars of the world's languages than any other force in history. Obviously these facts of cultural and linguistic pioneering conflict with the reputation of Christianity as one colossal act of cultural intolerance. This has produced a deep Christendom guilt complex, against which all evidence seems unavailing. It is important, however, to get people to budge because the default Christianity they now practice is a worn-out cultural fragment of something much greater and much fresher. We should still try to resolve the conflict by getting the facts out and by offering an interpretation that is consonant with the facts and that is equally persuasive. Open-minded people will see the point.

QUESTION 62: You keep surprising us with facts and figures, but I still think you underestimate the resistance of the West to the idea of Christian mission. The West is inclined to dismiss world Christianity by reducing it to Third World syncretism blended with vestigial paganism and spiced with exotic and implacable tribalism. The Christianity part is lost in that description. Are you aware of such attitudes?

ANSWER: Yes, I am, and that's why I appeal to sympathy and understanding of the hard facts at our disposal. I don't take people's agreement for granted. One cannot, for example, trust that people will necessarily appreciate the contradiction of saying flatly that Christianity stripped Africans of their culture but still left them saddled with tribalism, as you say. But, yes, I am not deluding myself about my chances of convincing too many people.

QUESTION 63: So what sustains you? Aren't you drained by the skepticism?

ANSWER: What sustains me is the sheer power of the story that is represented by the lives of the individual men and women whose faith and devotion reinforce the veracity of the apostolic witness. I have witnessed scenes of eager crowds pressing to get into the church, their only motivation being their irrepressible desire to be included in the fellowship of faith. I am moved by the strength and tenacity of their faith, and humbled by the knowledge of the obstacles they had to surmount in the process. So I am not drained by the skepticism of critics. Rather I am uplifted by the strength of the subject. I could go on, but it would take us further away from the subject.

Prognosis: Religion, Democratic Renewal, and Western Encounter

QUESTION 64: What is happening in Africa and China, for example, is what you must have had in mind when you talked about "the gospel in world history" in your introductory comments. Can you explain?

ANSWER: Yes, I can. I spoke about the implications of current Christian expansion for a fresh understanding of the gospel in world history — those words were too important for me not to have developed them further, and I'm glad for a second chance to do so now. A central affirmation of the gospel is that God was in Christ reconciling the world (2 Cor. 5:19), and you could argue that world history has been caught in the throes of the search for genuine communities of freedom, solidarity, and reconciliation. It is that search that the gospel has so well illuminated, and in some crucial ways in Africa has helped to promote against the odds.

I guess I can make the point in a different way by speaking of Christian expansion as an expansion not of denominationalism, with its sharp doctrinal disagreements and its narrow exegesis of Scripture, all braced with a certain attitude of entitlement, but of a growing historical consciousness that God is alive in history through the specificity of language, culture, and custom. Under natural circumstances people are afraid of the strange, the different, and the remote, and without faith in a common humanity they will suspect and reject one another. Even common language or common family does not necessarily create common understanding, as we know only too well from domestic conflict and family feuds. Faith and trust, however, can allow proximity and difference without fear or denial. We see something of this in the rich legacy of documentation of the world's languages that Bible translation has fostered. The language of faith and Scripture in Christianity is no different from the language of society, and in the systematic documentation of the world's languages Christianity contributed to global awakening through local renewal. The world is becoming one, not from the synthesis of all cultures into one, or from the discovery of a common genetic pool, but from the accelerating pressure to acknowledge and celebrate difference when that is no longer remote. That is the deep movement of the spirit in our time.

QUESTION 65: So the sowing of the gospel seed has not only produced what you refer to as unexpected abundance with expansion, it has also produced a qualitative change in the role we give to the local in terms of membership in the world community? Is that what you mean by world history?

ANSWER: You put it well. Human beings are made in the image of God, and Jesus in his defining Jewishness is the archetype of humanity's imperishable divine potential, the cosmic symbol of what God has ordained for us. History is impregnated with that spirit of ethnic authentication, and the gospel compels us to reimagine humanity in the specificity of God's reconciling work, to the end that humanity, nurtured in its fundamental mother tongue idiom, may experience a new birth of life, to the end that all God's children may have a second chance. No human being deserves to have his or her mother tongue denied, whatever the appeal of a lingua franca.

This theocentric notion of the equality of persons is the essential thread of the fabric of a free society based on the rule of law, and has been a major force in the rise of national communities in the West. The problem arose when similar national communities were envisioned, or imagined, if you will, for societies outside the Western experience. How such communities should develop without the tradition of individual liberty, freedom of conscience, and personal responsibility became a crucial question for the new international order, with numerous U.N. documents promulgated for the purpose. Yet, apart from their value as international festoons, these U.N. universal declarations had little effect on attitudes on the ground where hard-core ideologies from both the left and the right found ready soil. The fact that many of these societies happened to be preindustrial shows that ideology can take root in any society, so long as there is a predisposition for it.

You can see from this checkered picture how the person conceived as a free and valued partner in the work of God is central to the Western conception of national life. The work of God is more truly divine the wider the scope of the common good it achieves. Many societies that tried to evade this religious conception of human worth have had to pay a heavy price in political oppression, judicial arbitrariness, and social injustice. The rise of world Christianity has for that reason attracted suspicion and hostility from entrenched political leaders, and only ecumenical diplomacy, coupled with the talent to suffer quietly, has averted a worse fate for believers. It is still with good reason that world Christianity is suspected as a moral challenge to the political idolatry of the ideological state, whether imperial or secular. The ideological state has often felt driven by its scruples to attempt to thwart Christianity by "strangling the baby while it is still in the manger," in the vivid metaphor of one official reaction. Herod has allies in unsuspecting places even today.

QUESTION 66: Sobering thoughts, those. Yet at the risk of diverting you again from the worldwide character of Christian expansion, may I go back to my question (#50) and ask what you think people in the West can learn from world Christianity?

ANSWER: That's still a big question! Let me answer in two parts: First, the West should get over its Christendom guilt complex about Christianity as colonialism by accepting that Christianity has survived its European political habits and is thriving today in its post-Western phase among non-Western populations, sometimes because of, and often in spite of, Western missionaries. The religious strife and conflict that accompanied the political domestication of Christianity in Europe have not been repeated with the rise of world Christianity, and Europeans therefore should be assured that strife and conflict, and their accompanying territorial upheaval, need not follow Christian expansion. Furthermore, world Christianity is not merely an echo of globalization, though there is important overlap in certain sectors. On the contrary, in some instances new Christian movements are a reaction to the ravages and threats of globalization, with concerted attention to the value of local cultures and economies, the challenges of social dislocation and marginalization, the interests and dignity of families, and the importance of community well-being. World Christianity is evidence of a boundary-free global economy being witness to boundary-hinged communities of faith. The kingdom of mammon is too footloose to contend against the root claims of the kingdom of God.

Second, world Christianity offers a laboratory of pluralism and diversity where instead of faith and trust being missing or compromised, they remain intrinsic. You could not recognize world Christianity without the myriad tongues of praise and hope that also echo humanity's hopes and dreams. It shows that you don't have to be a religious agnostic in order to be a devout pluralist!

QUESTION 67: How can we in America do that, given our particular situation and church tradition?

ANSWER: By drawing on the lessons of Third World immigration into the United States. Along with this immigration has come a steady inflow of new religious movements from Latin America, Asia, and Africa. Korean and Hispanic populations, for example, have established new communities of faith across the country. They have created new styles of religious life and undertaken programs of ministry among their own people. They have also demanded a more responsive theological education than the one currently offered in mainline seminaries. All this calls for dialogue and conversation by crossing new borders with sympathy, understanding, and patience. A new ferment is astir in our midst, and we should seize the opportunity it presents of mutual exploration.

QUESTION 68: Are you suggesting that American Christianity should have a broader and deeper sensitivity?

ANSWER: Well, yes. And it should do that by drawing on its dynamic youth culture and its ever-growing pluralism and diversity. Christianity should not anywhere be about the refusal to change the old; it should be about the willingness to embrace the new. Perhaps we could start with drawing on the great spiritual wealth of a free and generous nation, on community and neighborhood partnership, and on a commitment to justice and forgiveness. Those values may be regarded as the fruits of the Spirit. It is the primary responsibility of Christians to cultivate the Spirit in Scripture, devotion, and service, even though there is open access for all to the fruits of that devotion. The sky is the limit in this sphere, though others better equipped than I must take the lead. It is inevitable, and not always a bad thing in itself, that Western scholars should process the information about world Christianity through existing categories of policy questions; yet when it's all said and done, it would be derelict to allow the cold war habits of global menace to loom so large on the canvas of world Christianity that we lose contact with the facts on the ground.

Part III: Assessment and Feedback: Prelude to the Future

QUESTION 69: We've covered a lot of ground in our conversation, and it might be useful to track where we've been. Do you agree?

ANSWER: Yes, I agree.

QUESTION 70: You began by presenting the data on world Christian expansion, explaining how intellectual barriers have obstructed how the information is received. In all that you thought people's commitment to tolerance and pluralism makes them feel they should be unsympathetic to events in world Christianity. There are too many reminders of a discredited colonial past in world Christianity to make people comfortable with the subject, you indicated. Is that an accurate account of your view?

ANSWER: Yes.

QUESTION 71: You said you wanted to address this issue of colonial suspicion not by dwelling on the evidence, which in your view is unassailable, but by taking up the issue of attitude and assumptions. In that approach you wished to stress the postcolonial and surprising indigenous roots of current Christian expansion and growth. You said you were unpersuaded of the view that world Christianity is merely a continuation of the medieval imperial phase of the religion as "Christendom" (#3, 4, and 5 above). As I understand it, you want to make a distinction between "world" and "global" as they relate to Christianity on the grounds that world Christianity has nothing of the global structures of power and economics that global Christianity presumes. World Christian expansion, you said, has been occurring in societies with weak states and among impoverished populations, and there has been no global orchestration of this expansion. Do I represent you correctly?

ANSWER: Yes.

QUESTION 72: Against that global view, you put a great deal of emphasis on the indigenous dimension of world Christianity, saying the affected cultures experienced a renewal from the Christian encounter, the motives of missionaries notwithstanding, and that the renewal helps highlight elements that shaped the origins of the NT church (#8 above). You thought by paying attention to the indigenous roots of world Christianity that the modern West, otherwise so far removed from the environment of the NT, could gain insight into the nature of Christian origins. Am I correct in saying that you see such possibilities for reciprocity between the West and Third World Christianity?

ANSWER: You are correct.

QUESTION 73: You also observed (#14 above) that nothing is more indicative of the indigenous theological advantage than the adoption of indigenous names for God in Bible translation and their introduction into Christianity. You said we could test the veracity of this statement by noting how renewal movements in world Christianity have in the main been restricted to societies where the indigenous name for God was preserved, with corresponding minimal Christian impact in places where the name of God has been forgotten or suppressed. That, you claimed, constituted the indigenous theological advantage in world Christianity. You were not, I thought, suggesting that Christianity was completely interchangeable with indigenous religions, but that their theological compatibility allows Christian engagement to produce results that have indigenous credibility rather than just foreign approval. In your argument (#25 above) this view occupies a central place, doesn't it?

ANSWER: Yes, it does. And you represent it fairly.

QUESTION 74: In the discussion we spent a good amount of time dealing with the perspectives of a post-Christian West on world Christianity. We dealt with the skepticism, the mood swing (#13 above), the suspicion, the stereotype, the mistrust, and the plain disenchantment that at present afflict the modern West, a skepticism that shows itself in Western reports and studies on world Christianity. We suggested that the missionary propaganda of an earlier era has been replaced by a secular propaganda that is hostile to the Third World in its Christian phase, and that in both cases what counts is the propaganda or the hostility, and not the facts on the ground. Secular distrust of Christianity in general, for example, has stood in the way of giving Third World Christianity in particular any notice, just as missionary ideology stripped it of any value. In both cases the West speaks and others listen, or are supposed to. This may be the reason you spoke about wanting to shift attitudes rather than about relying on the evidence to do the necessary persuading (#62-63 above). And yet you still believe, don't you, that world Christianity offers the occasion for a meeting of minds between the West and the Third World?

ANSWER: Yes, I most certainly do. A post-Christian West is not so far gone that it cannot make live contact with a post-Western Christianity.

QUESTION 75: Interested in this meeting of minds (#53 above), you say we should explore between and among us the implications of Christian expansion abroad for the democratic renewal of society, because the value Christianity places on the individual will and the primacy of conscience in decision making, and on the free person as a valued partner in the work of God, had a formative influence on the rise of national communities in the West, with similar possibilities for other societies. You were not implying by this, I thought, that other societies be Christianized, for you did not say that national identity was a guarantee for religious faithfulness any more than colonial hegemony was advantageous for the gospel, but merely that the seeds of individual merit and human dignity are not the monopoly of any one society and should have a chance to grow and flourish everywhere. In other words, the soil that typically fosters freedom and allows the fruits of the gospel to abound has existed in societies that never had the tradition of exclusive territorial Christian rights. Your remark about God having preceded the missionary, I thought, made this point well, and it may also be related to your argument about the indigenous theological advantage, if I may bring that up again, in the sense of local renewal taking place without global orchestration (#41-44 above). In any case, you feel that religion has a role to play in the strengthening of public life and institutions, don't you?

ANSWER: Yes, I do, especially Christianity as a preferential option for the poor.

QUESTION 76: Of a piece with that line of argument is your contention that privatized piety is a cut-down religion that cannot meet the needs and challenges of a developing society, that the European habit of seeing religion as a social indiscretion (#53 above) evades a good deal of what the worldwide Christian resurgence is about, and that, furthermore, the secular account of the end and purpose of human life gives a misleading view of our human potential. Although I realize you have not elaborated on this point of view on the grounds, perhaps, that it belongs to another stage of the subject of world Christianity, am I right to think that you do not much care for religion as gnostic individualism?

ANSWER: You are. I'm not a child of Plotinus.

QUESTION 77: Which then leads me to ask: You're not a card-carrying materialist either, are you?

ANSWER: That's correct. I don't see myself as a dialectical commissar.

QUESTION 78: That's helpful to hear you say that. I should then surmise that your notion of religion as a dynamic phenomenon has more in common with empirical fact and practice than with philosophical theory and ideology, in part because you don't think it's helpful to look at religion merely as a doctrinal system or even as Scripture, and in part because lived experience carries more weight with you than speculative thought. The practices of religious people, you say at several points (#8, 18, 23, 53 above), can be as illuminating as systematic reflection, though less often utilized. You insist you are unwilling to draw a sharp line defining Christianity unless it is a line that connects and grows (#40). That's why you argue that to speak of the indigenous discovery of Christianity is more revealing than to speak of the Christian discovery of indigenous societies (#46 above). You stress the importance of faith in a personal God rather than faith in a theory or a system. You make a strong pitch for a personal God as the ruling power in the religions of Africa, pointing out that evidence for such a personal God exists independently of any commensurate political organization or economic system (#41, 50 above). You do not say this is because of special revelation à la Karl Rahner, but it fits well into that scheme. You pack a great deal of substance into this part of our discussion, and I feel I need to go over that ground carefully to make sure I have kept in step with you. You don't mind my doing that, do you?

ANSWER: Go for it. It's good to know that we're listening closely to each other.

QUESTION 79: The sticking point in all this, if you don't mind my saying so, is the allergy of a secular West to any suggestion of a return to Christianity. Memories of the painful religious wars of the sixteenth and seventeenth centuries, deepened by guilt over slavery, colonialism, and the Holocaust, have all but shut down all paths of a return to Christianity, except, that is to say, as a privatized subjective option. The heart, you said, is the toughest part of the body (#54 above), and in our case people have given their hearts to materialism and individualism. The West as a modern progressive society is committed to live as if God does not exist, *etsi deus non daretur,* or at any rate to live with no sense of the devil. Scientific advance has blown the cover of God and the corresponding moral absolutism. I can understand, in this environment, why you would be very circumspect about predicting a convergence between a post-Christian West and a post-Western Christianity. The gap may simply be too great in spite of the optical illusion of historical concurrence: a post-Christian West and a post-Western Christianity are historical contemporaries, but their kinship is not even skin deep. In a way you're right to suggest that the massive recession evident in a post-Christian West is a sign that we have entered a transition to the equally massive advance in a post-Western Christianity as the next phase of the serial development of the religion (#25 above). You said as one region of Christian impact declines, another region rises to take its place, like a relay race in which fresh energy is drawn from the reserve to sustain the momentum. The resistance of the secular West, however, does not seem to be wearing thin in spite of your caution against measuring the potential of world Christianity by the declining religious fortunes of a secular West. Do I understand you correctly when I say that you are not too optimistic about breaching the walls of this secular resistance?

ANSWER: Correct. I am not too optimistic. Hopeful is a different matter, for there are signs that human contact can buck stereotypes and complacency, as the Maasai example shows.

QUESTION 80: I notice that a good deal of your confidence in the prospects for world Christianity rests on the advances already made in Africa but also in those now promised in Asia, particularly in China (#56-59 above). In that connection your point about more languages being used in prayer, worship, and the reading of Scripture in world Christianity than in any other religion in the world is striking. In the West that fact is counterintuitive, for people think of Christianity not as a pluralist religion but as monocultural and unifocal and, to be honest, not even as a world religion. Denominational fragmentation plays a part in Christianity's cultural domestication in the West. But if I understand your position, you would say that the process of acute indigenization to which the religion has been subject in the world ignores not denominational boundaries and doctrinal claims as such, but their narrow exclusiveness. The same forces that have allowed the religion to strike root in traditional societies that do not know the claims for the limits of reason have confronted the churches with tasks of translation, adjustment, interpretation, and implementation that have in common indigenous momentum and personal motivation. World Christianity, you argue, is not the creature of impulses originating in the West, but is the result of mother tongue mediation and local response. It is a fresh impression that reveals a facet of the unfolding design of the gospel in its apostolic conception (#47 above). Is that what lends a sense of vindication to your confidence?

ANSWER: I couldn't put it better.

QUESTION 81: But don't get carried away just yet. I'll tell you where I'm stuck. In making the helpful distinction between global Christianity, or Christendom, and world Christianity, you note the volatility of church-state relations in the history of the West and underscore that with the striking weakness of political structures in areas of world Christian resurgence. Yet you call attention to the value of the religion in projects for democratic renewal and the strengthening of public life and institutions. I see that as a gap in your argument, unless, that is, you wish to separate Christianity from the power interests of the ideological state, whether imperial or secular. Is that your intention?

ANSWER: Yes.

QUESTION 82: Then how can Christianity assume a public role without proposing a doctrine of state sponsorship, something that would turn the clock back to doctrinal intolerance and cultural insensitivity? People in the West are not able to separate religion from politics in their minds, in spite of constitutional separation. Consequently, when they hear of Christian resurgence, they think not of divine largesse but of the recrudescence of hateful division and descent into intolerance. The facts of the case as you set them out cannot break this linkage in people's minds, as you acknowledge. The skepticism functions for secular people like a protective valve against the deluge of fanaticism. He that dies pays all debts, as would the demise of Christianity. That's why the new fact of world Christianity elicits the old fear of fanaticism. It's a case of guilt by association. You give only suggestive hints on this matter, I realize, but surely it is the crux of the secular resistance to the religion, is it not?

ANSWER: Yes, such a vision of Christianity causes the knee-jerk reaction you describe. Notwithstanding that, I try to make a case for religion promoting a moral conditioning of society such that democratic institutions can take root and flourish. Human beings as valued partners in the work of God, I argue, are necessary and indispensable in such an unthreatening political culture (#64-65 above). There's no reason why we should be fearful of such a prospect. I don't think I said — though I could have said — a lot more than that.

QUESTION 83: I think your point about the inconsistent demand for world Christianity simultaneously to promote collective discipline to stem moral decline and to support individual freedom with its potential for nonconformist behavior is a valid one. It is impossible in that situation to please conservatives and liberals at the same time. You can conclude from that, I suppose, that the church should not adopt an ideological direction for its teachings, however much it may have to trim its sails ac-

86

cording to the prevailing winds. The theocentric understanding of human worth for which you plead should be
an inseparable part of the church's vocation, though the
fruits of that conception of human dignity belong with
the public good. Did I get that right?

ANSWER: You hit the nail on the head.

QUESTION 84: May I be so bold as to say that the
kind of open-minded discussion we have been engaged
in here encourages me to think that people on both sides
of the religious question have much to gain from honest
dialogue. If that is what you mean about freeing ourselves from ideological constraints and encountering the
world in the spirit of mutual exploration, then I'm all for
it. Agreement is not necessary for that kind of mutual exploration — indeed, a certain degree of disagreement is
essential to keep the parties honest. Do you agree?

ANSWER: Most wholeheartedly.

QUESTION 85: I notice the irony of the fact that one
may have to agree to disagree. It is the mirror image of
the other irony you spoke about in your opening comments of the holes in the blanket inclusivism that *ex-
cludes* Christianity. At any rate, you would say that we
should all invest in building bridges and in strengthening confidence in our mutual capacity for understanding
and respect. World Christianity, you plead, is entitled,
and hospitable, to such gestures of mind and spirit, and
that we should not settle back, or be encouraged to settle
back, into old habits. The top-down culture of Christendom, with social pedigree ruling the roost, has been replaced by the bottom-up shakedown that world Chris-

tianity has induced. Non-Western Christians have as such been dealing with matters of fundamental Christian identity and discernment concerning what it means to belong to a new faith community. They are doing so, according to you, in political, cultural, and religious settings that are volatile, diverse, complex, highly fluid, and in a climate of sustained interfaith encounter (#17 above). In the midst of the upheaval, people have found a new sense of being challenged, grounded, and affirmed, haven't they?

ANSWER: Yes, they have.

QUESTION 86: Was there one figure from the past who might be a symbol of the current ferment in world Christianity, someone who, responding to the upheaval of his or her time, took a bottom-up view of church and society?

ANSWER: Yes, there was, and it was Bishop Ajayi Crowther (ca. 1807-91), who was born in Nigeria in the year, it turned out, the slave trade was abolished by the British Parliament. Your question provides the opportunity to let him have the last word, as is appropriate. The boy Crowther was captured in his village by Muslim slave raiders who sold him to a slave merchant in Lagos. From there he was taken on a slave ship bound for Brazil. Miraculously he was rescued off the high seas by the British Naval Squadron and disembarked in Freetown, a settlement founded in 1787 for the purpose of settling freed slaves. Crowther rose rapidly to assume leadership among his fellow freed Africans. He saw a natural role for himself as an antislavery campaigner, surrounded as he was by the ravages of the slave trade at the source and supply end in West Africa. He had impeccable credentials for that, having just, as it were, come back from the dead. Facing down the chiefs who conspired with slave captains to maintain the human traffic, Crowther, with meaning, invoked as his own the words of the ancient prophet: "For Zion's sake will I not hold my peace, and for Jerusalem's sake I will not rest, until the righteousness thereof go forth as brightness, and the salvation thereof as a lamp that burneth" (Isa. 62:1). He led the campaign to suppress the trade in Nigeria, traveling extensively for that reason well into his eighties.

QUESTION 87: By the way, the name Crowther must have been adopted, right? At any rate, my question is, what role can one assign to Crowther in the story of world Christianity? Did Crowther's missionary vocation affect his capacity for cultural sensitivity? Did his understanding of religion allow him to be inclusive and tolerant of others? I recognize that I'm trying to evaluate him by standards of our own time rather than by those of his, but, I guess, that's the risk you run when you try to shift current attitudes by means of past examples. Slavery, for example, is not the burning issue for us that it was for Crowther and his contemporaries, and so they faced a different challenge. Today, however, cultural sensitivity, diversity, and inclusiveness are primary issues for us, and accordingly, they become the only way we relate to the past (#66 above). So I press with my question: How did Crowther measure up to these standards?

ANSWER: Yes, the name was adopted from his English missionary sponsor. By virtue of his site investigations long before field anthropology was a recognized branch of scholarly work, Crowther mapped the course of the indigenous discovery of Christianity. He showed remarkable cultural sensitivity specifically in his pioneering work in African language development, in interethnic collaboration, in Bible translation — his Yoruba Bible of 1851 was the first in an African language — in sensitive study of African religious ideas and practices, and especially in interfaith relations with Muslims at a time when the Victorian age was far less enlightened on that subject. Muslims, accordingly, honored him by giving him the title of imam, an Islamic office. Crowther was equally forward-looking in promoting Protestant-Catholic collaboration in the mission field, setting an example by donating land for the fledgling Roman Catholic mission that was then just entering Nigeria. Even by our more prickly standards, Crowther was exceptional.

QUESTION 88: That seems self-evident. There must have been other Africans equal to Crowther. I imagine they were very well received in a Victorian age desirous of making blacks into surrogate Europeans (#32, 62 above) — not that Crowther saw himself that way. The point is, how did the European world respond to such success stories?

ANSWER: The Victorians were offended that Africans should think they were the equals of Europeans rather than take their place in the low order of nature. The prevailing ideology of inferior or lesser races raised a barrier against African advancement, and the emerging anthropology reflected the ambivalence by giving the prevailing colonial ideology respectable backing. Sir Richard Burton, an experienced traveler in Africa and a founding officer of the Royal Anthropological Institute in London, and Edward Tylor (1832-1917), considered the father of cultural anthropology in the West and the first academic professor in anthropology at Oxford in 1884, for example, represented this rejectionist attitude. Crowther and his Creole compatriots were vilified by Burton and others as half-reclaimed barbarians clad in dishcloths, inferior specimens, savvy niggers, hybrid and uppity Africans, effete and degenerate, their Krio patois an omnium-gatherum of the debris of inferior dialects standing in the way of education and civilization even though, ironically, education and civilization were begrudged the Creole Africans in question.

QUESTION 89: How, in heaven's name, did Crowther respond to these aspersions?

ANSWER: Crowther refused the bait. By nature and disposition he was a guileless man. Still, he was deeply disappointed by the fact that the ad hominem abuse was diverting attention from the important struggle against slavery and from the encouraging work of indigenous moral transformation. He regretted the personal attack, but he bore it *ad finem* with inborn grace and charity.

It is, however, instructive to recall the work of an anthropologist whose views on native cultures were a great deal more positive. This was Robert Henry Codrington (1830-1922), a contemporary of Tylor whose lectures at Oxford he once attended, and later a missionary in Melanesia from 1871 to 1888. A student of the local language and culture, Codrington cautioned against the rootless generalizations of his fellow anthropologists and called for the need to reject armchair pronouncements and to hear the people's "own account of themselves." In other words, a need to respect the indigenous voice in cultural study. It was echoed in the call of Bronislaw Malinowski (1884-1942) in the 1920s for anthropologists to test their doctrines "in the crucible of practical reality." Malinowski invented the technique of "participant observation."

QUESTION 90: I now fully appreciate why you are committed to changing minds and attitudes (#55, 62 above), since proof of ability failed to overcome prejudice even in Crowther's day. And what you describe of him makes him a figure of global significance, using "global" not in the controversial orchestrated sense. How did Crowther fit into this dual identity as a child of Africa and as a commissioned agent of a religion with a worldwide reach? Do we know enough details of his life and work to make that judgment?

ANSWER: Crowther's dual identity served him well. It fitted so well with the role demanded of him by historical circumstances as well as with his natural talent. His life and work helped advance the acute indigenization that carried Christianity forward and transformed it into its post-Western phase. The wealth of detail we possess on his life was, by virtue of his own sense of vocation, a lived embodiment of the gospel, a personification of Christianity as it crossed borders from its old chosen Western medium to its new Gentile rehabilitation. Our knowledge of his life allows us, even inspires us to track the genesis of world Christianity at a significant point of its indigenous inception and personal appeal. The world scope of the religion received validation from the local roots it so deeply struck in society and in personal experience. Crowther, reflecting that, raised it to a new level of national commitment. He had an uncanny sense of the historical irony of Christianity as a colonial ruse for native exploitation and as a moral stratagem for national empowerment at the same time. There are sharp clues in that irony about the upsetting implications of local empowerment for Christianity's colonial agenda. Crowther's story adds a compelling human touch to a religion that set out full of boisterous imperial clamor but became in the field an ironic source of resistance against slavery and of local empowerment against colonial subjugation. Less than that would be enough to make us rethink our attitudes.

CHAPTER TWO

Christianity Reappropriated: The Bible and Its Mother Tongue Variations

Part I: Translation and Renewal: The Holy and the Commonplace

Whether in everyday, literary, or liturgical Latin, Christians introduced words and phrases drawn from ordinary speech and occasionally from Greek. The novelty arose both in language and style. The Old Latin versions of the Bible, which drew heavily on colloquial usage, influenced speech patterns among Christian communities, and this linguistic phenomenon, reflecting in turn the often low social origins of the converts, allowed a measure of freedom within the restrictions of the literary language. Notions of genre were similarly affected. Christian "literature," that is, stories from the Bible, dealt by and large with topics that did not fit into the classical oratorical divisions. Their forms of expression were

95

"humble" but their matter "sublime." . . . The Bible, or its translations, attempted to make God's word accessible to all, no matter what the level of education. . . . The blending of classical stylistics and biblical themes greatly influenced the development of medieval Latin and Romance languages.

BRIAN STOCK[1]

When he's not answering the phone he studies French so that he can talk to St. Thérèse, the Little Flower, when he goes to heaven. Mr. Logan tells him very gently he might be on the wrong track in this matter, that Latin is the language you need in heaven and that leads to a long discussion among the boarders as to what language Our Lord spoke, Peter McNamee declaring for a fact it was Hebrew. Mr. Logan says you might be right there, Peter, because he doesn't want to contradict the man who brings the Sunday meat home on a Friday night. Tom Clifford laughs that we should all brush up on our Irish in case we run into St. Patrick or St. Brigid and everyone glares at him, everyone but Ned Guinan who smiles at everything because it doesn't matter one

1. Brian Stock, *The Implications of Literacy: Written Language and Models of Interpretation in the Eleventh and Twelfth Centuries* (Princeton: Princeton University Press, 1983), 22-23.

way or the other when you're dreaming of the horses in Kildare.

FRANK MCCOURT[2]

Being the original Scripture of the Christian movement, the New Testament Gospels are a translated version of the message of Jesus, and that means Christianity is a translated religion without a revealed language. The issue is not whether Christians translated their Scripture well or willingly, but that without translation there would be no Christianity or Christians. Translation is the church's birthmark as well as its missionary benchmark: the church would be unrecognizable or unsustainable without it. Consequently, the more Christians press for a return to the origins of their religion, the more they stumble unreassuringly in the gap between the infinitely varied languages adopted for Scripture and worship and the language in which Jesus preached. Since Jesus did not write or dictate the Gospels, his followers had little choice but to adopt a translated form of his message. The missionary environment of the early church made translation and the accompanying interpretation natural and necessary. Mission in that sense was liberating, just as rejecting it was regressive.

If we view Christian origins in the light of the trans-

---

2. Frank McCourt, *'Tis: A Memoir* (New York: Simon and Schuster, 1999), 129-30.

lated milieu of the church, then we come upon a remarkable point with respect to the history of religions. Christianity seems unique in being the only world religion that is transmitted without the language or originating culture of its founder. In the early centuries of the Christian movement Scripture played a major role in Christian formation, community nurture, and institution building. The apostolic epistles, written mostly on the fly, became timely standards of instruction and interpretation, and were an effective instrument for ensuring a measure of unity amidst the resulting diversity of styles and emphases. Still, there was a lot of splintering as rival or dissenting communities of believers searched for idioms and patterns made necessary by each fresh situation and encounter.

Whatever the language, Christians found themselves propelled toward a popular mode for translation and for communicating the message. The general rule that people had a right to understand what they were being taught was matched by the view that there was nothing God wanted to say that could not be said in simple everyday language. God would not confound people about the truth, and that made the language of religion compatible with ordinary human understanding. The gospel proclamation stripped religious discourse of the hocus-pocus and elevated the voice of the *Volk*.

Christian authorities in later centuries might oppose such populist, subversive implications of translation, the notion of popular access being a threat to the power and control they felt entitled to. But for anyone so interested, a clear-cut case existed of the necessity of translation, and so long as the church was spreading and growing, the matter of popular access could not be suppressed entirely. Christianity could avoid translation only like water avoiding being wet.

As it happened, in the centuries of ferment and expansion, Christians became pioneers of linguistic development with the creation of alphabets, orthographies, dictionaries, and grammars. The resulting literacy, however limited, produced social and cultural transformation. A culture that for the first time possessed a dictionary and a grammar was a culture endowed for renewal and empowerment, whether or not it adopted Christianity. The fruits of Christian labor on this matter were undiscriminating. The benefits of mother tongue literacy spread without precondition or preferment, with the rule of popular access inducing a commensurate process of local awakening. Given the long and well-documented history of vernacular translation in Christianity, it is staggering to think how much work in studying vernacular translation still remains to be done on the subject.

When we contrast such vernacular translation with, for example, the pattern of Islamic missionary expansion, we discover a rich field of comparative investigation. Islam is comparable in range of impact even though it refrains from translating its scripture for the prescribed acts of worship and devotion. The many translations of the Quran that exist lack canonical authority for that reason. Muslims may use the translations for private study, but not for the stipulated acts of public worship, and certainly not as a substitute for the original. Attempts to do otherwise have failed. That Islam should spread as well as it does and still preserve the Quran in the original Arabic makes for a fascinating study in contrast, and illuminates a crucial feature of the temper of Christianity as a religious dispensation. Without a counterpart to the revealed Quran of Muslims, Christians transmitted their Scripture in the languages of other people, indicating thereby that these languages have a priority in the Christian scheme. This is more than just a tactical concession to win converts. It is, rather, an acknowledgment that languages have intrinsic merit for communicating the divine message. They are worthy of God's attention.

Christians quickly enough became accustomed to thinking of revelation not primarily in terms of the arcane and the recondite, even though they were familiar with Delphic oracles and gnostic secrecy, as Basilides of Alexandria testified, but in terms of koine and the Vulgate, of country speech and popular diction. Traditionally the hallowed language of religion is designed to mystify, to intimidate, to incriminate, to overwhelm, and to induce a mood of guilt and moral peril. A recognized trait of religions is encouraging a superstitious tendency in their followers to like best what they understand least. That made sincerity in the religious life an elusive commodity.

In his plain use of religious discourse, however, Jesus departed radically from that tradition. He taught his disciples to follow his example by employing a simple and direct use of language: let your communication be yes or no (Matt. 5:37), a teaching later recalled for general adoption (James 5:12). Jesus disfranchised the forked tongue. Paul, though formed in the habit of sealed knowledge, came clean ultimately by embracing Jesus' teaching. He took up the subject of common, impartial access with lyrical eloquence (1 Cor. 1:17, 20; 2:6; 14:6ff.; 2 Cor. 1:12). God does not dissemble or vacillate, nor should God's witnesses. "As surely as God is faithful, our word to you has not been Yes and No." Jesus Christ was not God's Yes and No, but all the promises of God find their Yes in him (2 Cor. 1:17-22). Paul appealed to the rule that with God there is no respect of persons, race, or learning (Rom. 2:11; 3:1; 1 Cor. 1:20). That is why the *book* in Christian usage connoted sincerity in oral communication (1 Cor. 5:8; 2 Cor. 1:12; Titus 2:7), and not textual sophistry, as Galen, the Greek philosopher, pointed out in criticism. Bitten by the criticism, theologians, however, obliged by cultivating the art of the complicated and the abstruse, and, heaven help us, making religious learning befuddling, whether in order to impress or to intimidate, it made little difference. But Jesus taught that the authority of the text might not be used as a pretext for evading the plain import of common sense. Pilate expressed the tragic stubbornness that written authority can exercise on those in power when he declared in grim desperation, "What I have written, I have written" (John 19:22). Jesus rated spiritual deafness, not illiteracy, among the greatest impediments to receiving the gospel (Matt. 13:19ff.); he flailed at the religious teachers of his

day for their misuse of written authority and for misleading the poor, the simple, and the ignorant (Matt. 23:13ff.;
Luke 11:42ff.). The spoken word, Jesus challenged,
should be formed of the wholesome seed and partaken
with an understanding heart, a rule we should, with
profit, apply also to the pulpit. (The people demanded: "If
you are the Christ, tell us plainly" [John 10:24]; "I have
spoken openly to the world. . . . I have said nothing se-
cretly" [18:20].)

The church managed to keep alive the flame of popular piety in the transition between the collapse of the Roman Empire and the rise of the great monasteries. Rhetoric and grammar, and sometimes jurisprudence, still
exercised a fascination for the learned, such as Boethius,
Cassiodorus, Fortunatus, Felicianus, Florentius, Flavius
Felix, Coronatus, and so on, but church practices, inspired by ascetic faith, enthroned the popular medium.
Gregory the Great (d. 604) was a patrician by birth
though he later came under ascetic influence. He became pope in 590. Gregory cultivated simplicity of style
and, considering them sterile verbiage, rejected the
showy ornaments of rhetoric. His work represented a
break with the classical style. Asceticism caused the rup-
ture with the classical style by recalling the church to its
mission, thus leading it to the people.[3] It was its missionary life that allowed the church to employ literature as an
instrument of popular culture.

3. Henri Pirenne, *Mohammed and Charlemagne* (1939; reprint,
London: Unwin University Books, 1968), 128.

As one historian affirmed, the force that changed and revived Latin literature came from Africa, the Latin of Septimius Severus, ancestor of the emperor, of Tertullian, of Cyprian whose African name was Thascius, and of Augustine, whom Julian of Eclanum called the "African sophist." The Latin of Christianity was stripped of the conceits of rhetoric and made accessible to people in a vulgarized version. To write Latin for the people the church made vulgar Latin into a living tongue. The simplicity of language broke the conventional barrier between spoken and written language. Even when scientific subjects were treated in learned works, the goal was to make them accessible to the people, as the work of Isidore of Seville (d. 636) illustrated. There was not the slightest feeling in all this work of seeking to recover or maintain adherence to a revealed language, for none existed for Christianity. Cyprian, for example, could write at length about the Eucharist without using the word, so opposed was he to Greek, the originating language.

Christians may be excused for feeling confused about what language Jesus spoke, because in the long centuries of translation and the indigenization process that went with it, nearly every major language, and many minor and obscure ones, were adopted for Scripture and worship, making it hard to recall the point of departure. From that pluralist perspective, no one language had primacy over another, and no person might be denied access to God on account of the language he or she spoke. It is this rule of universal access that the history of Bible translation has promoted, sometimes with uneven results, admittedly; often with embarrassing cultural shibboleths reflecting European notions of entitlement, undoubtedly; and not so rarely with naive confidence in the task, it has to be confessed, but always with reference to the receiving cultures. That has obvious implications for the history of the affected cultures, whether or not they became Christian.

At any rate, prevailing Christian practices and the speed of passing centuries caused people scarcely to remember what language the founder of their religion spoke, as if that mattered not a whit. In its place Christians arrogated that privilege to the language most natural to them. That's how for the church fathers the Greek Bible stood as the authoritative Scripture, so much so that when Jerome in the fourth century produced the Latin Vulgate from the Hebrew text rather than from the prevailing Greek Septuagint, he was attacked as endangering church teaching. A riot broke out in Tripoli when his translation of the book of Jonah was read publicly. Augustine warned him of dangerous division in the congregations if his translation was allowed to go forward.[4] But that translation, with the endorsement eventually of the Council of Trent in 1546, later became *the* Catholic Bible. That process of acculturation was repeated for English speakers in respect of the Authorized Version of the Bible, commonly called the King James Bible. That Bible went Trent one better when it acquired an apocryphal reputation as the only Scripture Jesus knew!

4. C. White, *The Correspondence between Jerome and Augustine of Hippo* (Lewiston, N.Y.: Edwin Mellen Press, 1990).

Christianity has felt so congenial in English, Italian, German, French, Spanish, Russian, and so on, that we forget it wasn't always so, or we inexcusably deny that the religion might feel equally congenial in other languages, such as Amharic, Geez, Arabic, Coptic, Tamil, Korean, Chinese, Swahili, Shona, Twi, Igbo, Wolof, Yoruba, and Zulu. Our cultural chauvinism makes us overlook Christianity's vernacular character. It is telling, for example, that the translators of the King James Bible in the seventeenth century saw fit, even after Tyndale and Coverdale, to defend their bold action against those opposed to translation by asserting, "For is the Kingdom of God become words or syllables? Why should we be in bondage to them, if we can be free?"

The opposition to English as the prerequisite language of Scripture and worship had roots in secular society, with the universities in England as the academic holdout. It was only in the twentieth century that English at long last gained academic respectability with the establishment of departments of English. Typically the syllabus added Old English as a safeguard. It would be enough to make Tyndale's ashes glow in disbelief. (The first such department, created in the eighteenth century, was, revealingly, in the United States at Harvard University.)

Because of the changes wrought earlier by religion, secular attitudes shifted away from viewing the vernacular as undignified. The fact of Christianity being a translated, and translating, religion places God at the center of the universe of cultures, implying free coequality among cultures and a necessary relativizing of languages vis-à-vis the truth of God. No culture is so advanced and so superior that it can claim exclusive access or advantage to the truth of God, and none so marginal or inferior that it can be excluded. All have merit; none is indispensable. The vernacular was thereby given the kiss of life.

It was only their theological scruples that allowed Christians to view Bible translation as a scandal. They overlooked the obvious fact that no one was pretending that the Gospels had ever existed in the tongue of Jesus. A new situation has risen today, however, and Bible translation into the mother tongue has opened the way for the worldwide Christian renewal and for the diverse cultural expressions that have become the vintage mark of the religion as a global phenomenon, suggesting the need for a fresh theological outlook to take in the changes.[5] The missionary linguists who shouldered the burden of translation grappled with numerous technical issues of alphabet, script, text, tone, orthography, grammar, semantics, usage, culture, and currency, matters of great importance to specialists, it has to be stressed. Yet it was in the indigenous reception and appropriation of the gospel in the postcolonial era that the magnitude and scale of what was achieved was finally revealed. Without any of the doctrinal conflicts of sixteenth-century Europe that splintered the Bible into ecumenical shrapnel, Bible translation in the modern missionary movement made ample the heritage of linguistic pluralism and turned

5. In this connection see Lawrence Venuti, *The Scandals of Translation: Towards an Ethics of Difference* (London: Routledge, 1998).

Christianity into the possession of the worldwide human family. The name of Israel in translation, as tribe, nation, and vocation, moved the lips of the world's children with glad songs of peaceful Zion.

Surprisingly negative attitudes about Bible translation, however, still persist among people, religious or not. One widespread attitude is that Bible translation is dishonest: it is done with motives of gaining converts, not helping local people. Another is that it violates the rights of people not to have their languages and cultures tampered with by missionaries. It is often accused of corrupting cultures by introducing foreign and artificial words and concepts. The translated Bible, critics say, is a colonial tool that weasels its way into native cultures to subvert and exploit them. It is an unwarranted intrusion into what people hold dear and true. All this righteous indignation begins to suggest, one might think, a favorable view of Islam and its untranslated Quran, yet Islam's rejection of translation seems at odds with the mother tongue franchise of Bible translation. One or the other makes a religion colonial, translation or nontranslation, not both.

At any rate, given the strength of feeling on Bible translation and the wide-ranging objections raised, it would be useful to deal with the matter in steps. For that I will adopt a question-and-answer style to help with focus, direction, clarity, movement, and economy in presentation.

Part II: The River and Its Tributaries: Theme and Continuities

Catholic and Protestant Soundings

QUESTION I: Does not the fact that veneration of the Bible has been made into a Protestant ideological cause make translating it a sectarian enterprise? Wasn't the idea of *sola Scriptura* of the Protestant Reformation a loaded attack on Roman Catholicism? Would Bible translation not extend this controversy into other societies?

ANSWER: I accept that the Bible was a focus of controversy in the Reformation, although I'm not sure everything said then about the reasons for breaking with Rome could be attributed to the Bible. We should remember, for instance, that Erasmus, a contemporary figure, stoutly defended Bible translation even though he remained a Roman Catholic. In any case, your point is that the *sola Scriptura* claim perpetuates the spirit of sectarianism in non-Western societies, and my answer is that these societies would bring their own very different experiences to bear on the transmission and reception of the Bible. Bible translation in fact revealed a greater distance between sixteenth-century Europe and indigenous societies of later times. Thus, apart from a common commitment to produce the Bible in the vernacular, Luther in Germany and Crowther among his Yoruba people have precious little else in common. But I accept your point that Bible translation became, from the nineteenth century, a Protestant specialty until recent times.

QUESTION 2: But you cannot deny that the *sola Scriptura* principle inspired false confidence in the Bible as a moral panacea, can you?

ANSWER: That's two questions in one. The *sola Scriptura* principle did call attention to the authority of the Bible, but as to the idea of the Bible giving you everything you wanted, that's a different issue. *Sola Scriptura* in fact left missionaries unsighted with respect to much in the culture that was not directly related to Bible translation, and that prevented excessive interference with wider cultural processes. Commentaries and related biblical aids, for example, were left out, and with them the Western intellectual tradition associated with the Enlightenment. Bible translation was a shelter for indigenous ideas and values.

Culture, Innovation, and Tradition

QUESTION 3: Isn't it a fact that Bible translation warps indigenous cultures by imposing on them the inflexible constraints of a written Scripture?

ANSWER: Actually, the opposite seems to have happened, with Bible translation stimulating the indigenous narrative tradition by introducing stories of the Bible and stimulating the storytelling predisposition of the oral tradition.

QUESTION 4: Aren't you worried that translation compromises Christianity by opening the door to superstition and unwholesome practices? Translation is unfaithful to the true genius of religion, don't you think? It risks tinkering with the truth and turning it to our own advantage.

ANSWER: Yes, I can see the hazards, though your question is misdirected. Translation must be consistent with Christianity's religious genius for it to occupy the role it does. At any rate, your view of translation as a threat to an establishment view of the truth explains why institutional religion opposes it, Christianity not exempted. Riots erupted in Athens when, for example, the Revised Standard Version of the Bible was released. People there may not have remembered how the early church itself agonized over the issue of admitting Greek-speaking believers into the fellowship, so new was the idea then (Acts 11; 15). Many churches in the Catholic and Eastern tradition, in fact, have forbidden translation on pain of severe sanctions. While for liberal Protestantism Scripture is a text like any other, and should be treated accordingly. Yet the reason why translation has not been laid to rest is because Christians do not possess the Scripture in the language of the founder of their religion, and for new converts this demands receiving the message in their own tongue. Two thousand years later the idea of Christianity without a revealed language remains new, at once revolutionary and disconcerting for habituated Europeans, and exciting and empowering for new Third World believers.

Approaching the subject historically should help us focus on the effects and consequences of this fact on religion and society rather than trying to look, and perhaps not find, a theological safeguard for the idea of translation in the inaccessible mind of God. In the history of Christianity, Bible translation represents a revolutionary conception of religion as something translatable and ambi-cultural, and that fact people can recognize, whether or not they are religious themselves. As an ancient Christian source put it, any foreign culture is native to Christians and any motherland is foreign. It is a new turn in the history of religion, and translation embodies and promotes that. The church anywhere and everywhere is situated, *bon gré, mal gré,* in a translated environment, whether or not it practices translation itself. Pentecost, the church's adopted birthday, we may recall, occurred in Jerusalem, not in Bethlehem, Jesus' birthplace (Acts 2:5ff.).

QUESTION 5: Okay, let me take this historical view and ask you again whether you don't think the social effects of Bible translation are detrimental to indigenous cultures by prejudicing their imaginative capacity. Written Scripture, even in translation, is too confining for illiterate cultures, isn't it?

ANSWER: No, it's not. Bible translation inscribes into the cultural imagination a narrative and wisdom tradition that enhances oral and ethnic affinity with biblical stories of creation, covenant, captivity, wilderness, suffering, restoration, hope, and abundance. With the added advantage of a dictionary and a grammar, a culture's enhanced capacity to connect and to expand becomes cumulative. Without such advantage, a culture is at risk of stagnation, if not of failure.

Common Access and the Hidden Agenda

QUESTION 6: As far as religion is concerned, don't you think you're making too large a claim for translation? After all, however important, translation is only half the story, the other half being teaching people correct ideas about God, salvation, faith tradition, and the moral life. How do you answer this?

ANSWER: You're right, translation isn't everything. But it is a necessary and essential catalyst. Little can be achieved or imagined without it, including religious instruction.

QUESTION 7: I have to push you here. Don't you think translation diverts us from the real strengths of indigenous cultures, their aesthetic life in art, ritual symbolism, music, dance, dreams, and healing? Perhaps that's why these cultures held so tenaciously to their oral traditions in the face of external challenge.

ANSWER: I don't agree that Bible translation is a diversionary ploy, and here's why. Indigenous cultures rely on language as a living resource of the whole system of life — social, economic, political, and personal. Without its language a society is certain not to survive, except perhaps as a client culture. The nonverbal systems of ritual and aesthetics are imaginative extensions of the verbal form. It is in language that we find a rich storehouse of the people's wisdom as proverbs, axioms, precepts, and sayings.

QUESTION 8: Let me keep up the momentum by asking whether you don't think Bible translation is a clever decoy to bamboozle people into abandoning their values and way of life in favor of a foreign religion? Bible translation is cultural espionage by means devious and nefarious, is it not?

ANSWER: No, I don't think so. I can think of less laborious and less uncertain ways of forcing people to change their religion. Jihad, for example, is a proven alternative. The *mujáhid* scholar/warrior in that case holds all the cards in his hands, conceding nothing to the other side, including the idea that the enemy's language might have any scriptural merit. A comparable tradition in the history of the church was when Christendom adopted this jihad notion of religious change. All that was required for a whole people to change its religion was for the Christian ruler to say so. That was how, for example, Charlemagne converted the pagan Saxons: he issued a fiat, and they were baptized by platoons. If such conditions existed today, we would employ the drill and fire hose, not translation.

No, I think if you want to force religion on people, Bible translation is the last thing you'd think of. The demands of language and professional study, and the commitment to local forms and usage are inconsistent with coercing people and fixing the outcome. The linguistic and cultural skills required for translation are an acknowledgment that patient demonstration of religious claims and personal persuasion are indispensable, and their outcome unpredictable. The persuasive option, for that is what it is, does not imply repudiation, but a transformation of the old values and practices so that they may live on in the new life in fulfillment of the people's own deep yearnings and desires. The outcome is a matter for indigenous discernment and judgment.

QUESTION 9: Aren't you suspicious still that Bible translation was a weapon of spiritual colonialism in which missionaries disingenuously offered the people the Bible in their tongue, allegedly, but with the aim of taking away the original contents of their language? I repeat, mission was cultural invasion, and Bible translation was the stealth weapon of choice. Am I right?

ANSWER: The question you ask has tremendous staying power, no matter what I say here. So let me recognize that fact right away. The groans of subject races as they reeled under the yoke of the *encomienda* colonial system instituted in 1503 by Queen Isabella of Spain continue rightly to haunt us in all subsequent accounts of the European encounter with non-European societies in Latin America and everywhere else. Bible translation, as you point out, is also haunted by that specter, even though the method of translation deviates sharply from the method of conquest. To answer your question, then, the complaint of native subjugation would be justified had European theological commentaries and exegesis been made a requirement of Bible translation and mother tongue literacy, because those books are well stocked with notions implicit and explicit of European intellectual superiority and cultural ascendancy. Unlike the Bible, commentaries are designed for individual competence and study, not for the communal ear or for sharing, and thus represent a bias for textual authority. The oral culture would have suffered a fate little different from ethnic collapse had not the mother tongue intervened to avert the uncontested dominion of textual cosmopolitanism. Bible translation, accordingly, fosters a climate of choice and persuasion. It's what I tried to say on the *sola Scriptura* issue, if you remember (#1, 2 above).

Translation and Cultural Conservation

QUESTION 10: Your reference to commentaries and exegesis reminds me that I have an objection to Bible translation as being too simplistic. It perpetuates an anachronistic, prescientific worldview about creation, the virgin birth, miracles, bodily resurrection, life after death, the second coming of Christ, and judgment day as literal truths. Doesn't such a superstitious, crude picture of the universe perturb you?

ANSWER: No, frankly, it doesn't, I'm afraid to say. You won't mind if I'm up front on this, will you? On your specific point, Bible translation is faithfulness to the word of God, not loyalty to one or another worldview, and certainly not to an elitist account of the matter. The task itself is guided by the view of God's interest in all peoples and their cultures, not by whether or not these peoples accede to our standards of progress. The peoples of the world have a right to come to their own view of the matter. You were complaining just now about missionaries using the Bible as a stealth platform to advance their own agenda. Shouldn't you, to be consistent, complain just as

vehemently if we use the Bible to promote the Enlightenment agenda of rationality? Because that would be stealth
invasion no less.

QUESTION 11: I can't believe you have an answer for
everything, so let me cut to the chase and be provocative.
I'm prepared to make a distinction between the missionary agenda, which, I admit, I don't like, and the Enlightenment agenda, which I like and would like to see spread
all over the world, trust me. That's the kind of mission I
support. Christians could sign on as theologians of the
hermeneutics of suspicion or liberation, or whatever
other fancy name they wish to call it. You'd still be right
to criticize that as cultural intrusion by the West, but
you'd do so on the defensive. You'd do so on my turf. But
let's skip to another issue. Would you not agree that Bible
translation places illiterate societies at a massive disadvantage by confronting them with the idea of religion as
a book, a subtle code for standardization?

ANSWER: I also can't believe you have a question on
everything! But what you say here would be true only if
the Bible were nothing more than a general issue manual
on how to beat the competition. It could then prescribe a
certain level of proficiency as necessary qualification for
that. But the Bible is God's word, whatever the commercial motives behind its production and dissemination. In
representing God's interest and action on behalf of humanity, the Bible describes and proclaims the story of
God and its personal connection with the stories of the
peoples of the world. The Bible makes for community by
bringing pastoral attentiveness to bear on matters of fam-

ily, home, society, and church. Far from dividing the world between winners and losers in a standardized market, the Bible offers limitless space for personal improvement and cultural variety. The Bible is not just about willfully putting a book between religion and us, but rather it is our assurance that we can know God as one who speaks and woos us personally, not as one who writes and threatens us anonymously. Even theologians of your ilk should be able to live with that, I should think.

QUESTION 12: You are keen to defend indigenous cultures, I can see. In that case, aren't you troubled that Bible translation violates the rules of secrecy that bind traditional cultures by exposing mystery oracles and codes and thus destroying their power and effect? In many traditional cultures, as in Victorian society, religion is taboo to women and children. And yet Bible translation ignores those taboos by reducing things to the commonplace in a bid to achieve ease of comprehensibility, doesn't it?

ANSWER: Guilty as charged. In my defense I should, however, say that Bible translation does not so much destroy the power of religion as put that power into the hands of ordinary people, yes, especially women and children, in order that they may realize their highest potential. In the early church, we should remember, priests were typically recruited from the humble classes. Cyprian, however brilliant himself, was a novice when he was elected bishop, and he records the stories of bishops and clergy who were illiterate and who opted for the use of the "eyes of the mind" rather than of the eyes of the face for expounding Scripture. The unmarked Christian graves at Timgad and Sousse in North Africa, for example, move us more powerfully than the thrones of the mighty, and bear eloquent testimony to the role of ordinary folks in the church. Even popular speech patterns among Christians in medieval Europe influenced usage in the wider society, with the colloquial genre competing successfully with classical forms. The Bible helped engender an anti-elitist culture of open access, with a bias toward people of low social origins.

QUESTION 13: I'm not impressed. Doesn't the fact that Bible translation introduces choices and options in traditional cultures where none existed before represent an act of cultural willfulness?

ANSWER: That sounds like a sympathetic question, but it's not, if you'll allow me to say so. Choice and option are essential to being human and responsible. The Bible is not a preschool kit for ordaining childhood. Living is a high stakes contact sport, and involves making choices, from sunrise to sunset, from the cradle to the grave. Bible translation enshrines that fact by appealing to mother tongue affirmation as the basis for encounter in religion. Even if we differ about what constitutes an acceptable outcome, we should all agree that choice is a prerequisite for personal integrity. That's what Bible translation stands to demonstrate.

Translation, the Cultural Option, and Interfaith Encounter

QUESTION 14: If I may, I'd like to go back to your comments about the controversial nature of Bible translation even for churches in the West (#4 above), and ask whether you don't think translation is unacceptably sectarian in a world of other religions. For religious traditions that do not translate their Scripture, such as Islam, translation is an unnecessary obstacle to interfaith solidarity. If we can't stop it, shouldn't we at least restrict it?

ANSWER: I know many would like to find another way to be religious, even if that means bypassing the mother tongue because it's too varied. But such a choice imposes too high a price by minimizing humanity's rich diversity and difference. The logic of Bible translation, however, is that access to God should be compatible with mother tongue affirmation, that in matters touching on our ultimate worth and significance it is vital that we know, but not exclude, God by the accents of birth and family. We do not threaten one another by coming into God's presence with the variety of tongue and race that marks our humanity. It's when we turn our tongue and race into a god that we arouse the dragon. A little religion here is a dangerous thing. To turn to Islam, the fact that it does not translate its Scripture for worship and devotion does not necessarily insulate the religion against sectarian excesses or improve its capacity for interfaith friendship. There is no ready-made formula for that.

QUESTION 15: If you think translation of Scripture is

so important, why did a religion like Islam flourish without it? Doesn't that undermine your argument?

ANSWER: That's an important question with relevance to interfaith relations. Without making the translation of the Quran a centerpiece of its mission, Islam spread on the basis precisely of its untranslatable Scripture. Unlike the early Christians who contended against the principalities and powers (Rom. 8:38; Eph. 6:12; Col. 2:15), Muslims consecrated the sword and the state for the mission of Islam. There is no separation of church and state in Islam, and so religion and government may unite to advance and protect each other. For the early Christians, however, the two remained in tension, if not in conflict. Persecution, not rulership, was the norm of the day.

QUESTION 16: What about the Crusades in Christianity? Did not Christians use the sword and the state to promote religion?

ANSWER: The Crusades, late in time, were something of a coup d'état against the teachings of Jesus, against what the Quran would call his *balagh* [3:42; 54:4]. With the church's backing, European kingdoms looked upon Jerusalem as "Crown redeemer" territory. Religion became jurisdiction or rulership, and the exhortation to fight the good fight of faith (1 Tim. 6:12; 2 Tim. 4:7) in the spirit of the Suffering Servant and to contend against the principalities and powers (Eph. 6:12; Col. 2:15) was superseded by royal prerogative, by *Vexilla Regis*.[6]

---

6. Kenneth Cragg, *Am I Not Your Lord? (Alastu bi-rabbikum): Human Meaning in Divine Question* (London: Melisende, 2002), 100ff.

In contrast, the jihad tradition in Islam is neither an aberration nor a mere instrument of the state à la Clausewitz (d. 1831), the Prussian army officer who propounded the notion of total war in the cause of what is tantamount to political fundamentalism as state policy. Jihad was commitment to God's will, not "as in heaven so on earth," but "as on earth so in heaven" (Quran 33:36). It was a central religious office of the early Muslims, prescribed in scripture and in the conduct of the Prophet (Quran 4:76, 91f., 94f.; 8:70-71; 9:5, 29, 36, 41, 122; 47:4; 48:1-3). In the eleventh century a Christian concept of holy war was conceived in response to the Muslim doctrine of jihad: war against unbelievers was justified in the eyes of God. It backfired, and having whipped up bitter passions in the futile bid to recapture Jerusalem, the church set upon its own people in the Inquisition. The church, you may have forgotten, was born in Pentecost, while Islam was born in the *hijrah*, in the emigration to Mecca under a religious state. That year of the *hijrah* (622) is the birthdate of Islam as a religion and a state. Saladin (d. 1193), who captured Jerusalem in 1187 and defended it through the Third Crusade (1189-92), invoked the canonical tradition of jihad to rouse his fellow Muslims against the Christian infidels.

In the Muslim world, however, the Crusades, referred to as the wars with the Franks, were overshadowed by a contemporary event that shook the caliphal empire to its core. This was the Mongol invasion under Genghis Khan (d. 1227). The fact that Western Christians continue to harbor fresh remorse for the Crusades a thousand years after the events shows the Crusades to be a continuing embarrassment and a standing reproach to the church. No similar moral scandal attaches to Islamic conquests *(futúh)* then or at other times, for which credit is normally reserved for the sword of God *(sayf al-haqq)*. It is important to say here that much as the Christian wish to separate church and state might have been a response to the crisis of seventeenth-century Europe, the seeds were sown with the teaching and example of Jesus himself (Matt. 5:39; 22:21). A disaster like the Crusades showed the perils of departing from that teaching in a misguided bid to return to Christian origins, as I said at the outset. Bible translation belongs to a different moral world altogether. It may be a "crusade" of the word, if at all, but scarcely of the sword.

Translation and Competition

QUESTION 17: I obviously diverted you from the subject, but what you say about jihad and the idea of the Crusades is illuminating. To return to the subject, you must acknowledge that Bible translation is not the high-minded calling you make it out to be, but is driven by tawdry motives of gain and success. In which case, isn't it a fact that it has been a failure in many cultures? These cultures have in the main resisted conversion even though they have been given a translated Bible, cultures such as China, India, Japan, and the Middle East. That's proof that translation is not a guarantee for success, and should for that reason be abandoned, isn't it?

ANSWER: Translation, if you recall me saying, does not coerce or compel (#9 above). Rather, it puts in place a process whereby encounter in religion can take place through the idiom of the mother tongue. Translation guarantees nothing beyond the fact that an inculturated personal response is a necessary and legitimate basis for moral and social empowerment. Translation is not a tool for head-hunting. It merely argues for conversion by persuasion rather than by force or by anonymous means. Translation has no need of shibboleths. The decision to convert is one for the receiving culture, not for the translator, however well intentioned.

QUESTION 18: Given the all too evident reality of denominational fragmentation and rivalry, doesn't Bible translation play into the hands of sectarianism and naive fundamentalism?

ANSWER: Bible translation has been an extraordinarily broadening experience for the churches. It has facilitated ecumenical cooperation on an unprecedented scale, and has pushed the churches beyond their own safe cultural confines. It has challenged Christians to face people once considered exotic, alien, and remote, and made their idioms, prayers, hymns, music, and practices part of the heritage of the enlarged community of faith. It is no small accomplishment of Bible translation that Western churches have in their hymnbooks a selection of hymns and praise songs from other languages. Such translation work has mercifully helped to soften the hard tempers that were a legacy of Europe's intra-religious strife and subsequent colonial jingoism.

QUESTION 19: Hasn't Bible translation encouraged irresponsible amateurism in the church? People with little qualification in the field or with little knowledge of local conditions have been recruited and set loose with little guidance or oversight, and with little accountability to the local church. Can you defend that?

ANSWER: No, I can't and I won't. The many awful specimens of incompetence that exist make it clear the record is embarrassingly uneven. But, as Eugene Nida has shown in his *Customs and Cultures* (1954), some of the faults have been more on the clumsy and gratuitous than on the premeditated side, as a few examples will show. Missionaries in one place overeagerly translated Romans 3:23, "We have all sinned and come short of the glory of God," without realizing that in the particular language there was an exclusive as well as an inclusive "we." They had unwittingly adopted the exclusive form with the meaning, "We whites have sinned and come short of the glory of God." The villagers thought this referred to all the wrong things whites had done in their country, something they knew about very well without missionaries coming out to give it biblical reference. In a different example, a similar linguistic clumsiness led missionaries to translate the sentence in the Lord's Prayer, "Lead us not into temptation but deliver us from evil," as "Lord, do not catch us when we sin," a secret sentiment among the people who were now glad to have explicit biblical authority for it.

QUESTION 20: By peremptorily entering into a culture, missionaries are getting no less than they deserve. Did they learn their lesson and make adjustments?

ANSWER: They tried to, but often they were none the wiser for it. Take the example of those translators who anticipated trouble and tried to be proactive. One translator decided that the story in 2 Samuel 6:20 about Michal taunting David for dancing naked before God should be adjusted to accommodate the social indiscretion of nakedness. In the translation David danced in his underwear. For half a century missionaries in a region of East Africa had been saying, or thought they were saying, "The Lord be with thy spirit," without realizing that they implied, "Yes, the Lord be with your spirit, for we don't want him." Upon discovering their blunder, the dismayed missionaries rebuked their African friends for not correcting them. The Africans responded that they got used to hearing a great deal of strange things missionaries said in the local language, and put down the saying in question to that. A similar situation arose from the missionaries trying to translate the verse "Enter the kingdom of heaven." Lacking adequate language preparation, they rendered it incomprehensibly as "Go sit on a stick." Often missionaries confronted impossible linguistic hurdles.

QUESTION 21: But every culture has things that are peculiar to it and, as such, that defy translation. How, for example, do you translate for the seal-hunting Eskimos "Feed my lambs" (John 21:15), which presumes a culture based on farming and animal husbandry? Or for vegetarian Hindus, how do you talk about killing the fatted calf (Luke 15:23, 30)?

ANSWER: Yes, such cultural peculiarities are commonplace. They are what gives a culture its distinctive stamp. They constitute a challenge that dogs us all the time, reinforced by a priori norms or else by the presence of free-floating, unrehearsed cultural attitudes. A small child familiar with city life, for example, was asked to represent the story of the fall of Adam and Eve in the garden and their subsequent expulsion. The child drew the picture of a car with three persons in it, explaining that this was "God driving Adam and Eve out of the Garden of Eden." In such situations, however, an experienced translator would do a practice run with dynamic equivalents before committing to a final step.

QUESTION 22: All of that is evidence that translation is impossible, that language is a wonderful weapon for resisting foreign invasion, and that even linguistic experts cannot dent a culture's resolve to resist attempts at religious conquest. Yet you still defend Bible translation, don't you?

ANSWER: Yes, because in spite of such difficulties, translation is intrinsic to lived experience as well as being constitutive of Christianity's identity, whether or not it is done well. The translators of the King James Bible, for example, recognized how fundamental translation is to Christianity when they declared, "We do not deny, nay, we affirm and avow, that the very meanest translation of the Bible in English set forth by men of our profession . . . containeth the Word of God, nay, is the Word of God: as the king's speech which he uttered in Parliament, being translated into French, Dutch, Italian and Latin, is still the king's speech, though it not be interpreted by every translator with the like grace, nor peradventure so fitly for phrase, nor so expressly for sense, everywhere." Both successful and unsuccessful translations are judged such by indigenous criteria. A good translation vindicates local norms and standards; a bad translation fails for the same reason. Bible translation, thus, has a self-correcting mechanism built into the feedback.

On translation as an impossibility (*traduttore traditore,* "a translator is a traitor"), I think that's true only in a superficial or ironic sense. At bottom, if translation were impossible and languages were mutually exclusive, human beings would be condemned to living in Bantustans, with weak cultures at the mercy of strong ones. The divine capacity of language would in that situation be corrupted into a dogma of enmity. We deserve to be spared such a fate, whatever the human foibles of Bible translators.

Translation and Social Scale

QUESTION 23: All those arguments aside, an issue Bible translation cannot avoid is one of scale. The vast number of languages available makes it inconceivable that there are resources to match. That forces a practical choice about investing in languages with a critical mass and ignoring those that are economically unviable. Linguistic death is as inevitable as physical death. How does Bible translation take account of this economic reality?

ANSWER: We can look at the economics of translation in two ways. First, we look at the scale of what has been achieved, which is far out of proportion to the available finances. Motivation and skill had a lot to do with it. Second, we look at the correlation between the languages involved in translation and their economic importance. Some languages clearly had social and economic importance, but many more were remote and precarious. All this is to say that the practice of translation has not necessarily discriminated along the lines of economic advantage even if important economic consequences followed.

QUESTION 24: What about the political aspects? Doesn't the indiscriminate use of languages in Bible translation impede national unity and political integration? How can a Third World country with scarce resources, for instance, afford to allow universal access to the Bible to guide its planning and expenditure strategy? Is it safe to imbue people with the idea that every language has a right to an equal share of public funds? Wouldn't that make Bible translation guilty of mischief making?

ANSWER: It doesn't take much, you will appreciate, to incite political suppression of religion, and your line of questioning unwittingly begins to take us in that direction. That notwithstanding, we should say at the outset that the Bible is not a commodity, with translation a hedge fund, so to speak. Scripture is not designed to be peddled on the basis of market size and high yield. But the most critical issue in the terms you use to frame your question is the notion that the interests of national unity and political integration are best served by the suppression of difference and diversity and the promotion of linguistic uniformity and cultural conformity. But that begs the question: Whose language or culture should set the standard for uniformity and conformity?

We may have a genuine difference of opinion on this point, but I would argue that national development and social advancement are best served by harnessing the rich diversity and pluralism constituted by social and linguistic pluralism. Most people already speak more than one language, and Bible translation fosters the climate for that practice to increase. A national language policy, therefore, need not conflict with the practice of linguistic pluralism. A flourishing community, national or religious, is not an argument for imposing uniform practice and exclusive conformity. A sensible national policy must not squelch the talent for language, or for religion, by merely commodifying both.

Translation and Christian Unity

QUESTION 25: You have referred several times to the connection between Bible translation and forms of community practice. My question is whether the variety of language contexts does not create the conditions for fragmentation and schism. How can we ensure any remote notion of ecumenical unity if we give different languages a decisive role in religious practice?

ANSWER: That is a question lurking in much of what we've said so far, and I'm glad for the chance to deal with it explicitly, even if not fully here. I explained in my opening comments how Christianity is a translated religion because the Gospels themselves were a translated version of the preaching of Jesus, and that the missionary milieu of the early church necessitated further translations and, by implication, fresh adaptations of the faith. That is how, historically, Christianity spread across the world and penetrated cultures, a majority of which needed an alphabet. The significance of this historical feature of the religion is underlined when we remember the theological insight that the God we celebrate in the Christmas and Easter stories is available without hesitation or qualification in a language that is the people's own. Bible translation is a demonstration of that.

It follows from this theological insight that Christianity is not intrinsically a religion of cultural uniformity, and that in its historical expansion it has demonstrated that empirically by reflecting the tremendous diversity and dynamism of the peoples of the world. Christian pluralism is not just a matter of regrettable doctrinal splits and ecclesiastical fragmentation, but rather of variety and diversity within each church tradition. The difference now is that the world character of Christianity has expanded and deepened that pluralism for each faith tradition. Seen from the perspective of the river rising no higher than its source, this situation is not a failure of the religion but the triumph of its translatability. Bible translation enabled Christianity to break the cultural filibuster of its Western domestication to create movements of resurgence and renewal that transformed the religion into a world faith. Attitudes must shift to acknowledge this new situation. There is much to be gained by it.

Select Bibliography

Bediako, Kwame. *Christianity in Africa: The Renewal of a Non-Western Religion*. Maryknoll, N.Y.: Orbis, 1995.

Bredero, Adriaan H. *Christendom and Christianity in the Middle Ages*. Grand Rapids: Eerdmans, 1994.

Brenner, Athalya, and Jan Willem van Henten, eds. *Bible Translation on the Threshold of the Twenty-First Century: Authority, Reception, Culture, and Religion*. London: Sheffield Academic Press, 2002.

Cochrane, Charles Norris. *Christianity and Classical Culture: A Study of Thought and Action from Augustus to Augustine*. London and New York: Oxford University Press, 1957.

Cragg, Kenneth. *Am I Not Your Lord? (Alastu bi-rabbikum): Human Meaning in Divine Question*. London: Melisende, 2002.

Donovan, Vincent J. *Christianity Rediscovered: An Epistle from the Masai*. London: SCM Press, 2001.

Erickson, Paul A., with Liam D. Murphy. *A History of Anthropo-*

logical Theory. Peterborough, Ontario: Broadview Press, 1999.

Evans-Pritchard, E. E. *Theories of Primitive Religion*. Oxford: Clarendon, 1965.

————. *A History of Anthropological Thought*. Edited by André Singer. New York: Basic Books, 1981.

Faupel, J. F. *African Holocaust: The Story of the Uganda Martyrs*. London: Geoffrey Chapman, 1965. Rev. ed., Africa: St. Paul Publications, 1984.

Ferguson, John. "Aspects of Early Christianity in North Africa." *Tarikh* 2, no. 1 (1967).

Frend, W. H. C. *The Rise of Christianity*. Philadelphia: Fortress, 1984.

Goodpasture, H. McKennie, ed. *Cross and Sword: An Eyewitness History of Christianity in Latin America*. Maryknoll, N.Y.: Orbis, 1989.

Gray, Richard. *Black Christians and White Missionaries*. New Haven: Yale University Press, 1991.

Hastings, Adrian. *The Church in Africa: 1450-1950*. Oxford: Oxford University Press, 1994.

Hayashida, Nelson Osamu. *Dreams in the African Church: The Significance of Dreams and Visions among Zambian Baptists*. Amsterdam: Editions Rodopi, 1999.

Hitchens, Christopher. "A Man of Permanent Contradictions." Review of *The Long Recessional: The Imperial Life of Rudyard Kipling*, by David Gilmour. *Atlantic*, June 2002, 96-103.

Horton, Robin. "African Traditional Thought and Western Science." *Africa* 36, nos. 1 and 2 (1967).

Huntington, Samuel P. *The Third Wave: Democratization in the Late Twentieth Century*. Norman: University of Oklahoma Press, 1991.

Select Bibliography

Jenkins, Philip. "A New Christendom." *Chronicle of Higher Education*, March 29, 2002.

——. *The Next Christendom: The Coming of Global Christianity.* New York: Oxford University Press, 2002.

Johnson, Aubrey R. *The One and the Many in the Israelite Conception of God.* Cardiff: University of Wales Press, 1961.

Johnson, Luke Timothy, and William S. Kurz, S.J. *The Future of Catholic Biblical Scholarship: A Constructive Conversation.* Grand Rapids: Eerdmans, 2001.

Krabill, James R. *The Hymnody of the Harrist Church among the Dida of South Central Ivory Coast (1913-1949).* Frankfurt am Main: Peter Lang, 1995.

Latourette, Kenneth Scott. *A History of Christian Missions in China.* 1929. Reprint, New York: Russell and Russell, 1967.

——. *The Twentieth Century outside Europe: The Americas, the Pacific, Asia, and Africa: The Emerging World Christian Community.* Vol. 5 of *Christianity in a Revolutionary Age: A History of Christianity in the Nineteenth and Twentieth Centuries.* New York: Harper and Row, 1962.

Marwick, M. G. "How Real Is the Charmed Circle in African and Western Thought?" *Africa* 43, no. 1 (January 1973).

Mbiti, John S. *The Prayers of African Religion.* Maryknoll, N.Y.: Orbis, 1975.

Metzger, Bruce M. *The Bible in Translation: Ancient and English Versions.* Grand Rapids: Baker, 2001.

Moore, Hyatt, ed. *The Alphabet Makers: A Presentation from the Museum of the Alphabet, Waxhaw, NC.* Huntington Beach, Calif.: Summer Institute of Linguistics, 1991.

Nida, Eugene. *Customs and Cultures.* 1954. Reprint, Pasadena, Calif.: William Carey Library, 1986.

Nikkel, Marc R. *Dinka Christianity.* Nairobi: Paulines Publication Africa, 2001.

Norris, Frederick W. *Christianity: A Short Global History.* Oxford: Oneworld Publications, 2002.

Olson, Richard. *The Emergence of the Social Sciences, 1642-1792.* New York: Twayne Publishers, 1993.

Pirenne, Henri. *Mohammed and Charlemagne.* 1939. Reprint, London: Unwin University Books, 1968.

Rahner, Hugo. *Church and State in Early Christianity.* San Francisco: Ignatius, 1992.

Saitoti, Tepilit Ole. *The Worlds of a Maasai Warrior: An Autobiography.* Berkeley and Los Angeles: University of California Press, 1988.

Sanneh, Lamin. *Translating the Message: The Missionary Impact on Culture.* Maryknoll, N.Y.: Orbis, 1989.

————. *Encountering the West: Christianity and the Global Cultural Process.* Maryknoll, N.Y.: Orbis, 1993.

————. "Translation in Islam." In *Encyclopedia of Islam and Muslim Peoples.* New York: Macmillan. Forthcoming.

Shank, David A. *What Western Christians Can Learn from African-Initiated Churches.* Mission Insight series no. 10. Elkhart, Ind.: Mennonite Board of Missions, 2001.

Shenk, Calvin. "The Demise of the Church in North Africa and Nubia and Its Survival in Egypt and Ethiopia: A Question of Contextualization." *Missiology* 21, no. 2 (1993).

Smith, Edwin, ed. *African Ideas of God.* London: Edinburgh House Press, 1950.

Stackhouse, Max L., with Peter J. Paris, eds. *God and Globalization.* Vol. 1, *Religion and the Powers of the Common Life.* Harrisburg, Pa.: Trinity Press International, 2002.

Stackhouse, Max L., with Don S. Browning, eds. *God and Glob-*

alization. Vol. 2, *The Spirit and the Modern Authorities*. Harrisburg, Pa.: Trinity Press International, 2002.

Stackhouse, Max L., with Diane B. Obenchain, eds. *God and Globalization*. Vol. 3, *Christ and the Dominions of Civilization*. Harrisburg, Pa.: Trinity Press International, 2002.

Sundkler, Bengt, and Christopher Steed. *A History of the Church in Africa*. Cambridge: Cambridge University Press, 2000.

Takenaka, Masao. *Christian Art in Asia*. Tokyo: Kyo Bun Kwan, 1975.

Takenaka, Masao, and Ron O'Grady. *The Bible through Asian Eyes*. Auckland: Pace Publishing, 1991.

Ullendorf, Edward. *Ethiopia and the Bible*. London: Oxford University Press, 1988.

Venuti, Lawrence. *The Scandals of Translation: Towards an Ethics of Difference*. London: Routledge, 1998.

Walls, Andrew F. *The Missionary Movement in Christian History: Studies in the Transmission of Faith*. Maryknoll, N.Y.: Orbis, 1996.

————. *The Cross-Cultural Process in Christian History: Studies in the Transmission and Appropriation of Faith*. Maryknoll, N.Y.: Orbis, 2002.

White, C. *The Correspondence between Jerome and Augustine of Hippo*. Lewiston, N.Y.: Edwin Mellen Press, 1990.

Whitehead, Alfred North. *Religion in the Making*. Cambridge, 1927.

Wink, Walter. *Naming the Powers: The Language of Power in the New Testament*. St. Paul and Minneapolis: Fortress, 1984.

————. *Unmasking the Powers: The Invisible Forces That Determine Human Existence*. St. Paul and Minneapolis: Fortress, 1986.

————. *Engaging the Powers: Discernment and Resistance in a*

World of Domination. St. Paul and Minneapolis: Fortress, 1992.

World Christian Encyclopedia: A Comprehensive Survey of Churches and Religions in the Modern World. Edited by David B. Barrett, George T. Kurian, and Todd M. Johnson. 2nd ed. 2 vols. New York: Oxford University Press, 2001. Vol. 1, *The World by Countries: Religionists, Churches, Ministries.* Vol. 2, *The World by Segments: Religions, Peoples, Languages, Cities, Topics.*

World Christian Handbook. Edited by H. Wakelin Coxill and Sir Kenneth Grubb. London: Lutterworth, 1967.

World Christian Trends: AD 30–AD 2200: Interpreting the Annual Christian Megacensus. Edited by David B. Barrett and Todd M. Johnson. Pasadena, Calif.: William Carey Library, 2001.

Wyse, Akintola. *The Krio of Sierra Leone: An Interpretive History.* London: C. Hurst, 1989.

Xi, Lian. *The Conversion of Missionaries: Liberalism in American Protestant Missions in China, 1907-1932.* University Park: Pennsylvania State University Press, 1997.

Index